Dear Isaac

Happy birthday and
happy Christmas!!
Hope this inspires you to
explore our amazing world
with your Uncle Rara
love

Sarah
xx

# A WHOLE WORLD OF ART

## A TIME-TRAVELLING TRIP THROUGH A WHOLE WORLD OF ART

SARAH PHILLIPS

ILLUSTRATED BY DION MBD

**WIDE EYED EDITIONS**

# CONTENTS

**ALZENA**

# WE'RE GOING ON AN ART ADVENTURE...

Get ready, eyes open, brain alert, passport and pencils at the ready: we're off an *ART ADVENTURE*, all around the world!

Travel through *27 SCENES FROM ART HISTORY*, circling the globe with your two travel companions, *ALZENA AND MILES*. Look out for them on every page!

*OUR JOURNEY BEGINS 5,000 YEARS AGO*, when one of the greatest civilisations on earth was created by the Egyptians. On this journey, we will travel by foot, camel, elephant, ship, train, car and plane across *EVERY CONTINENT OF THE GLOBE*, and hear stories of some of the great artworks of the past. All artists emerge from and are shaped by the communities that they come from. In this magical super-tour you will *MEET REAL ARTISTS*, and learn about the world they lived in, from the buildings they saw and the clothes they wore, to the people they met and importantly *HOW AND WHY THEY MADE THEIR ART*.

Artists have always had a keen eye for finding the most interesting parts of our communities. Sometimes they work to order for the great leaders or organisations of their world; sometimes they work first for themselves and then work out how to sell their work. ART CAN BE MADE OF ANYTHING and paints, techniques and materials have changed rapidly over 5,000 years. New inventions and new understanding change the way we see the world, and like you, ARTISTS HAVE LEARNED HOW TO DO NEW THINGS ALL THE TIME.

Some hopes in our lives come around again and again: like the tide that washes in and out or the sun that rises and sets every day. As you travel across the planet and through time in this book, you will find SUBJECTS AND IDEAS that YOU MIGHT RECOGNISE IN YOUR OWN LIFE today. You'll also find plenty of things that look very different – but maybe these too can inspire you in your own artistic journey?

READY, STEADY, GO: THERE'S A WHOLE WORLD OF ART OUT THERE THAT IS JUST WAITING FOR YOU TO DISCOVER IT...

**MILES**

THE NEFERTITI BUST was found by a German archaeologist on the floor of a storeroom in 1912. It was taken to BERLIN, with the permission of the Egyptian authorities. Today, thousands of people travel to see it each year in the NEUES MUSEUM.

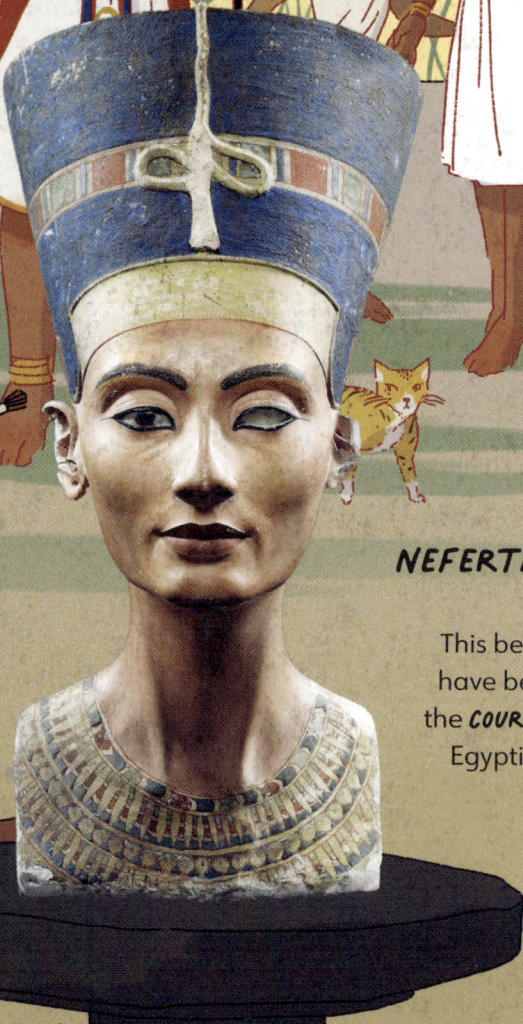

## NEFERTITI BUST, 1350 BCE

This beautiful head is thought to have been carved by THUTMOSE, the COURT SCULPTOR of the Ancient Egyptian Pharaoh, Akhenaten.

Nefertiti's long neck, high cheekbones, elegant eyebrows and HINT OF A MYSTERIOUS SMILE, have made her one of the most admired faces in art.

This work was carved from LIMESTONE and covered with a layer of PLASTER so that the artist could achieve more detail and a softer final effect. The NATURAL COLOURS add character and suggest movement making the sculpture still fascinating today.

Surprisingly, she only has BLACK QUARTZ in one eye. Some think this means the head was actually a MODEL rather than a finished work for display.

Since 1925, Egypt has *ASKED FOR THE NEFERTITI BUST TO BE RETURNED*. The bust of Nefertiti is one of many works from the African continent (in particular) that were taken and brought to Europe during the *COLONIAL ERA*.

In this *RELIEF SCULPTURE*, you can see Akhenaten and Nefertiti in a tender scene, holding their young daughters. The three girls all touch their parents as they sit beneath the rays and protection of *ATEN, THE SUN GOD*.

**AKHENATEN AND NEFERTITI WITH THEIR CHILDREN, 1340 BCE**

Little is known for sure about Nefertiti's life. Some say she took over as Pharaoh after her husband and that one of her six daughters eventually became the *WIFE OF PHARAOH TUTANKHAMUN*.

## 1350 BCE

# GIZA, ANCIENT EGYPT

### KEY ARTIST: THUTMOSE

THE REMARKABLE ANCIENT KINGDOM OF EGYPT LASTED FOR THREE THOUSAND YEARS: THAT'S FAR LONGER THAN THE TIME BETWEEN THE BIRTH OF JESUS CHRIST AND TODAY. IT BEGAN WHEN MAMMOTHS STILL WALKED ON OUR EARTH. THE EMPERORS OF THE OLD KINGDOM BUILT THE PYRAMIDS. THE ENORMOUS PYRAMID OF KHUFU AT GIZA WAS ORIGINALLY AN EXTRAORDINARY 147 METRES IN HEIGHT AND WAS THE TALLEST HUMAN-BUILT STRUCTURE FOR 3,800 YEARS! OVER TIME, THE OLD KINGDOM GAVE WAY TO THE MIDDLE KINGDOM AND THEN, AROUND 1570 BCE, TO THE NEW KINGDOM. THE FIRST DYNASTY OF THE NEW KINGDOM (THE 18TH DYNASTY OF EGYPT) WAS THE ONLY ONE BELIEVED TO HAVE WOMEN RULERS: HATSHEPSUT AND NEFERTITI. AROUND 1350 BCE, EGYPTIAN ART ADOPTED A NEW STYLE, A NEW RELIGION AND A NEW CAPITAL CITY UNDER THE RULE OF AKHENATEN AND NEFERTITI.

## 450 BCE

# ATHENS, GREECE

### KEY SCULPTOR: PHIDIAS

THE ARTISTS AND ARCHITECTS WHO BUILT THE TEMPLES AND STATUES OF ATHENS SET IN MOTION IDEAS OF BEAUTY AND HARMONY THAT WE STILL ADMIRE TODAY. HAVING DEFEATED THE PERSIANS, THE CITIZENS, LED BY THEIR RULER PERICLES, WANTED TO CELEBRATE THEIR SUCCESS AND GIVE THANKS TO THEIR SPECIAL GODDESS, ATHENA. THE EARLIER TEMPLE ON THE HIGH ROCKY SITE HAD BEEN BURNED DOWN BY THEIR ENEMIES, SO REBUILDING A BIGGER AND BETTER ONE WAS VERY IMPORTANT. THE FIRST IMPORTANT VICTORY OF THE GREEK FORCES AGAINST THE PERSIANS WAS THE BATTLE OF MARATHON WHICH GAVE ITS NAME TO THE FAMOUS LONG-DISTANCE RUNNING RACE. THE BIGGEST BUILDING, THE PARTHENON, IS ONE OF THE MOST FAMOUS EVER.

The Parthenon cost **469 SILVER TALENTS**. One talent was the fee to build one trireme: the most advanced warship of the era – so the building came at a price of more than an entire fleet of ships.

Athens was famous for its **DEMOCRACY** and **EVERY CITIZEN HAD A VOICE** and vote in how the city was ruled. The sculptor Phidias and his team carved more than 300 of his people in a long procession on the walls of the temple. He also carved pictures of the legendary battles between the **ANCIENT GREEKS** and the **CENTAURS**.

### VARVARKEION ATHENA, 2ND CENTURY CE

Athough the Athena statue from inside the Parthenon no longer exists, the Varvakeion is a **ROMAN COPY** of it.

Built of around **20,000 TONNES OF PENTELIC MARBLE**, the Parthenon must have sparkled under the brilliant blue skies. It was visible from many kilometres away and showed off the **STRENGTH OF ATHENS** as a warning to anyone wanting to invade.

The Parthenon housed a gold and ivory **STATUE OF ATHENA**. It was more than **12 METRES TALL**! The people of Athens admired her from the outside, from the hill of the Acropolis.

## THE PARTHENON, 442 BCE

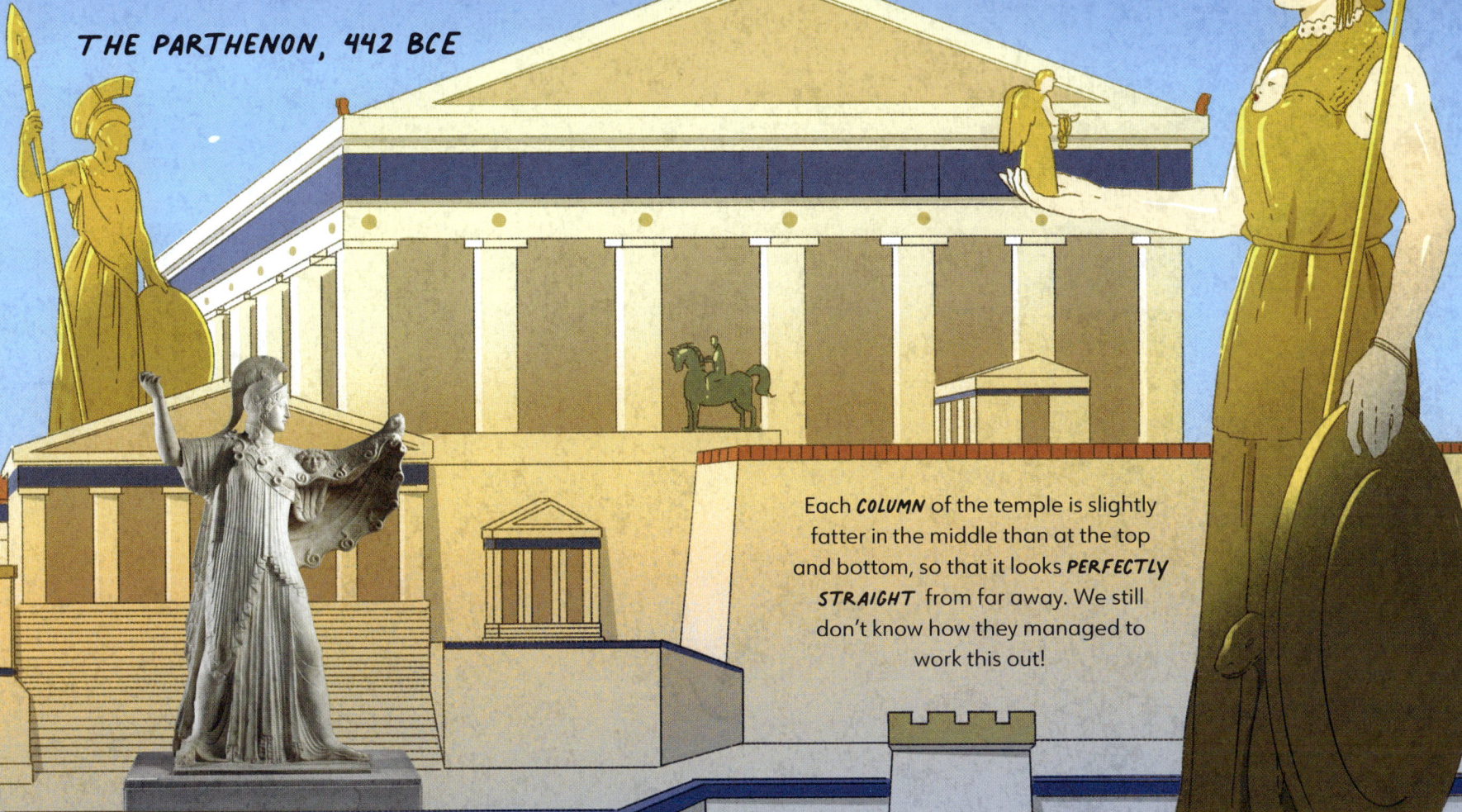

Each **COLUMN** of the temple is slightly fatter in the middle than at the top and bottom, so that it looks **PERFECTLY STRAIGHT** from far away. We still don't know how they managed to work this out!

**THE SCULPTURES OF ATHENS** were made by **PHIDIAS** – the most famous of all Greek sculptors and today there is an asteroid named after him.

The bronze Athena might remind you a bit of **THE STATUE OF LIBERTY IN NEW YORK**, but this figure was made more than 2,500 years earlier!

Outside the temple, there was another figure of Athena made from **BRONZE**. This 9-metre statue stood on the site for 1,000 years until it was taken away to Constantinople by the Romans. We are not sure what she held in her hand. What do you think would make a good symbol of power?

9

80 CE

# ROME, ITALY

IN 69 CE, ROME HAD FOUR DIFFERENT EMPERORS IN A SINGLE YEAR. THE LAST OF THESE, VESPASIAN, HEAD OF THE FLAVIAN FAMILY, WAS DETERMINED TO STABILISE THE EMPIRE AND BUILD THE LOYALTY OF HIS PEOPLE. HOW? BY BRINGING THE EXCITEMENT OF BATTLE AND THE TASTE OF VICTORY HOME TO THE ROMAN PEOPLE. INSTRUCTING HIS ENGINEERS TO PULL DOWN THE GOLDEN HOUSE OF THE HATED EMPEROR NERO, HE REPLACED IT WITH A FREE ENTERTAINMENT FACILITY IN THE CENTRE OF THE CITY FOR ROMANS TO ENJOY. THE WORLD'S LARGEST STADIUM HOUSED MORE THAN 50,000 SPECTATORS AT A TIME AND THE CROWDS ROARED THEIR APPROVAL AS THEY WATCHED MEN, WOMEN AND ANIMALS FIGHT IN FRONT OF THEM.

On the ground floor, *80 ROUND-HEADED ARCHES* framed with sturdy *DORIC COLUMNS* provide lots of entrances for everyone to get in and out quickly.

The Colosseum was built with *100,000 CUBIC METRES OF STONE* in just ten years.

Apparently, *EMPEROR VESPASIAN* himself sometimes appeared on the building site, carrying stones to encourage his teams of workers.

Vespasian paid for the building using money he had *TAKEN FROM JERUSALEM* during his time as an army general there. He put many of the *SLAVES* who were brought back from Jerusalem to work on the Colosseum, too.

*TITUS* only ruled for two years, before his brother, Domitian, became the last of the Flavian family to rule the *ROMAN EMPIRE*. Domitian ruled for fifteen years and continued the building programme of his father, dedicating the *ARCH OF TITUS* to his elder brother. On this detail from the arch, you can see the story of the *STOLEN TREASURE OF JERUSALEM* coming back to Rome as the soldiers carry the huge gold *MENORAH* from the temple above their heads.

THE COLOSSEUM, 72 CE

DETAIL FROM ARCH OF TITUS, 81 CE

Roman sailors pulled vast *SAILS* over the building to protect visitors from the hot sun.

Unlike earlier amphitheatres which were usually built into the hillside, the *COLOSSEUM STANDS ALONE* in the centre of the city. Engineers had to build some parts with *CONCRETE* and *RED BRICK* as a whole stone building would have crumbled under its own weight.

As the stadium was almost ready, the *VOLCANO AT MOUNT VESUVIUS* erupted, killing thousands and burying the towns of *HERCULANEUM* and *POMPEII* under ash. Titus earned respect by giving his own money to help those affected by the disaster.

11

750 CE

# TIKAL, GUATEMALA

LOST FOR ALMOST 1,000 YEARS, DEEP IN THE JUNGLE OF GUATEMALA, LIES THE ANCIENT CITY OF YAX MUTAL (NOW KNOWN AS TIKAL). ONCE THE HEART OF THE MAYA EMPIRE, THIS CITY HAD MORE THAN 3,000 BUILDINGS AND ITS CONSTRUCTION HAD BEGUN IN THE FOURTH CENTURY BCE. THE EXTRAORDINARY TEMPLE OF THE JAGUAR IS THE BURIAL PLACE OF THE 27TH MAYA KING, JASAW CHAN K'AWIIL I (ALSO KNOWN AS LORD CHOCOLATE) WHO RULED FOR AN AMAZING 52 YEARS. HAVING DEFEATED THE NEIGHBOURING STATE OF CALAKMUL, JASAW SET ABOUT BUILDING UP HIS CITY TO HONOUR THE GODS AND DEVELOP MAYA KNOWLEDGE OF ASTRONOMY, MATHEMATICS AND THE ARTS.

STELE 16, 711 CE

The Maya people played a ballgame with a *RUBBER BALL* – made from the gum of the *Hevea* tree.

This *'STELE'*, or *FLAT-STONE CARVING*, shows King Jasaw Chan K'awiil I dressed in *SYMBOLS OF POWER AND WEALTH*. It is hard to see details clearly now, but originally it would have been brightly painted.

The huge *KAPOK TREE* was sacred to the Maya people, linking the worlds beneath our feet, around us and the skies above. Tikal carvings often show amazingly detailed plants, which shows how much nature was valued.

By watching the sky, Maya priests learned about *ASTRONOMY* and developed a 365-day calendar. They used it to work out when to plant their crops and where to construct their buildings.

## TEMPLE OF THE JAGUAR, 750 CE

The nine steep levels of the temple represent the *NINE LEVELS OF THE UNDERWORLD*. Above them there is a final tenth step and then the temple. At the very top, 47 metres above the ground, is a spectacular roof comb.

The second biggest temple, the *THE TEMPLE OF THE MASKS*, on the site was built for his Queen who was known as 'Lady Twelve Baby Macaws'.

The Maya worshipped many gods at these ornately carved temples. There was *A GOD FOR EVERY ELEMENT OF NATURE* including the sun, moon, rainforest and flowers, which meant there was a deep respect for the natural world.

King Jasaw Chan K'awiil I was laid to rest inside the temple. His body was covered with *BEAUTIFUL OBJECTS*, including jade jewellery, shells, pearls, jaguar skins and painted ceramics.

13

*1010 CE*

# CHOLA EMPIRE, INDIA

LONG AGO, IN SOUTHERN INDIA, THE CHOLA DYNASTY WAS RULED BY RAJARAJA THE GREAT. UNDER HIS CONTROL, THIS HINDU EMPIRE EXPANDED SOUTH TO SRI LANKA AND NORTH TO THE RIVER GANGES. HE HAD HUGE INFLUENCE AND POWER ACROSS CHINA AND SOUTHEAST ASIA THANKS TO THE STRENGTH OF HIS SHIPS AND SAILORS. AT HOME, HE TURNED HIS CAPITAL CITY, THANJAVUR (NOW TANJORE) INTO A MARVEL OF ART AND ARCHITECTURE WITH ONE OF THE LARGEST BUILDING PROGRAMMES IN THE HISTORY OF THE WORLD. THE CHOLA DYNASTY LASTED ALMOST 400 YEARS AND THEIR ACHIEVEMENTS IN BUILDING, SCULPTURE AND PAINTING STILL AMAZE TODAY.

**THE BIG TEMPLE (BRIHADESWARA), 1010 CE**

Dance was hugely important to the Chola people and is a tradition that continues today. Some people call Shiva's dance in the Natarāja sculpture, *'THE DANCE OF BLISS'*. His *CALM SMILE* shows his ability to control the *FORCES OF THE UNIVERSE*.

More than 1,000 years ago, *LONG BEFORE THE INVENTION OF MACHINES*, Emperor Rajaraja the Great built the Big Temple (Brihadeswara). Dedicated to *LORD SHIVA*, it was the *TALLEST TEMPLE IN THE WORLD*, at an astonishing 66 metres high.

On the top of the tower is the bulging shape of *THE KUMBAM*. This crown is carved from a single rock and weighs 80 tons. Just over 1 kilometre away, archaeologists have found the beginning of a ramp which they think was used by *ELEPHANTS* to push the enormous rock into place.

The sculptors of the time also created many versions of the *NATARÂJA*: *SHIVA AS LORD OF THE DANCE*. No one else in the world could make *SOLID BRONZE* figures like this – at this time, or for many centuries afterwards.

The whole temple is made from one of the *HARDEST STONES IN THE WORLD: GRANITE*. But Rajaraja's skilled craftsmen still managed to carve thousands of figures all over the temple by hand.

In this sculpture, Shiva dances on top of *THE IMP OF IGNORANCE* you can see under his foot. At the same time, he beats the *DRUM OF CREATION* in one hand, unleashes fire to cleanse the earth and holds another hand up to reassure us.

NATARÂJA, 1010 CE

15

1250

# PARIS, FRANCE

CROWNED WHEN HE WAS JUST TWELVE YEARS OLD, LOUIS XIV OF FRANCE WAS SEEN AS AN IDEAL MEDIEVAL KING. DEDICATED TO HIS COUNTRY AND HIS FAITH, HE WANTED TO BE THOUGHT OF AS THE LEADER OF THE CHRISTIAN WORLD AS WELL AS KING OF THE FRENCH. UNDER HIS CONTROL, THE NUMBER OF PEOPLE IN PARIS GREW HUGELY AND HE LED TWO RELIGIOUS WARS. BY THE TIME OF HIS DEATH IN 1270, THE SORBONNE, THE UNIVERSITY FOUNDED DURING HIS LEADERSHIP, WAS WELCOMING STUDENTS FROM ALL OVER EUROPE AND 101 DIFFERENT CRAFT GROUPS HAD BEEN ESTABLISHED. HIS MOST FAMOUS ACT WAS TO BUY THE CROWN OF THORNS (BELIEVED TO HAVE BEEN WORN BY JESUS CHRIST ON THE CROSS) AND TO BUILD THE EXTRAORDINARY SAINTE CHAPELLE TO HOUSE THIS PRECIOUS TREASURE.

For Louis and the people of Paris, the fabulous art and architecture in the *MODERN GOTHIC STYLE* was both an *INSPIRATION* and an *EDUCATION*.

The chapel is on an island in the middle of the *RIVER SEINE* and was built right next to the King's palace.

Built in the *HIGH GOTHIC STYLE*, the upper chapel is a kaleidoscope of glorious colour in 15 amazing stained-glass windows which soar upwards underneath a roof of heavenly stars.

The windows show *SCENES FROM THE BIBLE*, from the Old Testament to the New, and ending with the arrival of the holy treasure in Paris for the king, who was later made a saint.

King Louis had another special treasure: *THE CRUSADER BIBLE*. It shows stories of the kings and leaders, especially David, who was an important role model for Louis, and is dressed in the clothes of the time.

The *STAINED GLASS WINDOWS* show over 1,000 figures across an area bigger than two tennis courts!

The craftsmen who made the windows used *FIVE COLOURS*, all came from *ROCKS AND METALS*. Blue from cobalt, yellow from antimony, purple from manganese and red and green from copper.

**THE CRUSADER BIBLE, 1250**

**SAINTE CHAPELLE, 1250**

The roof has *POINTS* around the edge to remind us of *JESUS'S CROWN*.

It is thought that at least six artists worked together to produce this bible. It shows us lots of detail about *LIFE IN THE 13TH CENTURY* as well as stories you may already know. This page shows Noah and his family in the ark.

The **FIRST RULER** of the Mali Empire was **SUNDIATA KEITA**, known as the **LION KING** – and the hero of the story later made famous by Disney. Unable to walk as a child, his mother, Sogolon, fled with him when their lands were taken by a cruel king. In 1235, Sundiata returned to defeat the Sosso king and **LIBERATE** the Mandinka people.

THE MANDEN CHARTER, 1236

Sundiata laid the foundation for a powerful and wealthy empire and proclaimed the first ever **CHARTER OF HUMAN RIGHTS**: the Manden Charter. This promises peace, respect, education and food security: ideas we are still striving for today.

Mansa Musa I came to power in 1312 CE, after the previous king, Abu Bakr II, disappeared at sea. He made his country rich by *EXPANDING TRADE* and mining *SALT AND GOLD*.

Under Mansa Musa I, *BOOKS* became the *MOST VALUABLE COMMODITY* in Timbuktu. Thousands of ancient manuscripts on arts, science, law, medicine, nutrition and astronomy were treasured in the *WORLD'S FIRST LIBRARIES*.

*THE CATALAN ATLAS* was created in 1375 by Spanish map makers. It is said to be the most important map of the middle ages. It shows *MANSA MUSA I* sitting on a throne, holding a nugget of gold in one hand and a golden staff in the other.

As well as mosques, Mansa Musa I built schools, universities and the *GRANDEST LIBRARIES IN ALL OF AFRICA*. These buildings are made from mud brick and the people of the city come together each year to repair them by hand after the rains.

# 1330
# TIMBUKTU, MALI

FOR HUNDREDS OF YEARS, WEST AFRICA WAS HOME TO THE GREAT MALI EMPIRE. THIS ANCIENT KINGDOM SPREAD ACROSS THOUSANDS OF KILOMETRES ALL THE WAY FROM THE SAHARA DESERT TO THE ATLANTIC OCEAN. IN THE 14TH CENTURY, MANSA MUSA I RULED THESE LANDS AND BECAME POSSIBLY THE RICHEST MAN IN THE WHOLE OF HISTORY. HE GAVE MUCH OF HIS MONEY AWAY, BUILDING WONDERFUL MOSQUES ACROSS THE REGION AND TRANSFORMING HIS HOME CITY OF TIMBUKTU INTO A HUGELY IMPORTANT CENTRE OF LEARNING FOR THE ISLAMIC WORLD.

## 1420

# BEIJING, CHINA

### KEY ARTIST: BIAN WENJIN

AFTER THE MONGOLS WERE DEFEATED, THE MING DYNASTY CAME TO POWER IN CHINA, AT FIRST UNDER THE RULE OF EMPEROR HONGWU. IN 1402, THE FOURTH OF HIS 29 SONS BECAME THE NEW EMPEROR AND WAS NAMED YONGLE. HE MADE BEIJING HIS CAPITAL CITY AND BUILT THE EXTRAORDINARY FORBIDDEN CITY AT ITS HEART. HE SENT THE FAMOUS EXPLORER ZHENG HE OUT ACROSS THE WORLD IN ENORMOUS SHIPS AND ENJOYED THE PRECIOUS THINGS HE BROUGHT BACK. CHINESE PORCELAIN BECAME FAMOUS EVERYWHERE AND THE MING PEOPLE REBUILT AND EXTENDED THE GREAT WALL OF CHINA TO DEFEND THEIR LANDS.

In painting, the best artists were very talented, known for their skills in *POETRY* and *CALLIGRAPHY* (painting in letters) as well as *PAINTING*.

At this time, *CHINESE MING PORCELAIN* reached a level of perfection never seen before. The pure smooth surface was made even more beautiful by extraordinary *RED* and *BLUE GLAZES*. Cobalt blue came from Iran and the red was made from copper.

The *PORCELAIN FACTORY* in the South at Jingdezhen made astonishing work for the Imperial court, with more than *TEN WORKERS* thought to have been involved on the production of a *SINGLE PIECE*. This shows how art has always been about more than a single individual!

The **GREAT WALL** stretched over 8,800 kilometres – it can even be seen from the Moon! It was Yongle's way of making sure the Mongols didn't return to take Ming lands.

Almost all the roofs in the Forbidden City have **YELLOW TILES** just for the Emperor. But the Library has a **BLACK ROOF** to symbolise water and its ability to protect against fire. The Crown prince's rooms had a **GREEN ROOF** to symbolise nature and new growth.

*BAMBOO AND CRANES, 1426-35*

The **FORBIDDEN CITY** is the largest palace in the world. The city was the **HOME OF THE EMPEROR** for more than 500 years and is thought to have needed one million workers to create the 9,999 rooms on its 72-hectare site.

This painting is a **HANGING SCROLL**, which would have been opened up only on special days. The **CRANE** is a symbol of immortality and the **BAMBOO** is typical of China too.

The artist who painted this scroll, **BIAN WENJIN**, became a court painter to **EMPEROR YONGLE** and his paintings of birds and flowers became famous across the Ming Empire.

COULD YOU MAKE YOUR OWN HANGING SCROLL? TAKE A CARDBOARD INNER TUBE AND TAPE SOME PAPER TO IT. CAN YOU PAINT THE BIRDS OR FLOWERS THAT YOU CAN SEE IN YOUR GARDEN OR PARK?

In sculpture, *DONATELLO* had an amazing ability to show feeling. His most famous work is the sculpture of the boy shepherd David who killed the giant Goliath in the Old Testament story. The work *CELEBRATES HIS YOUTH* and slender body as he holds the enormous sword of the giant in one hand and puts his opposite foot on his head. Just like today, the people of Florence loved a story where the *UNDERDOG WAS TRIUMPHANT*!

DAVID, 1440

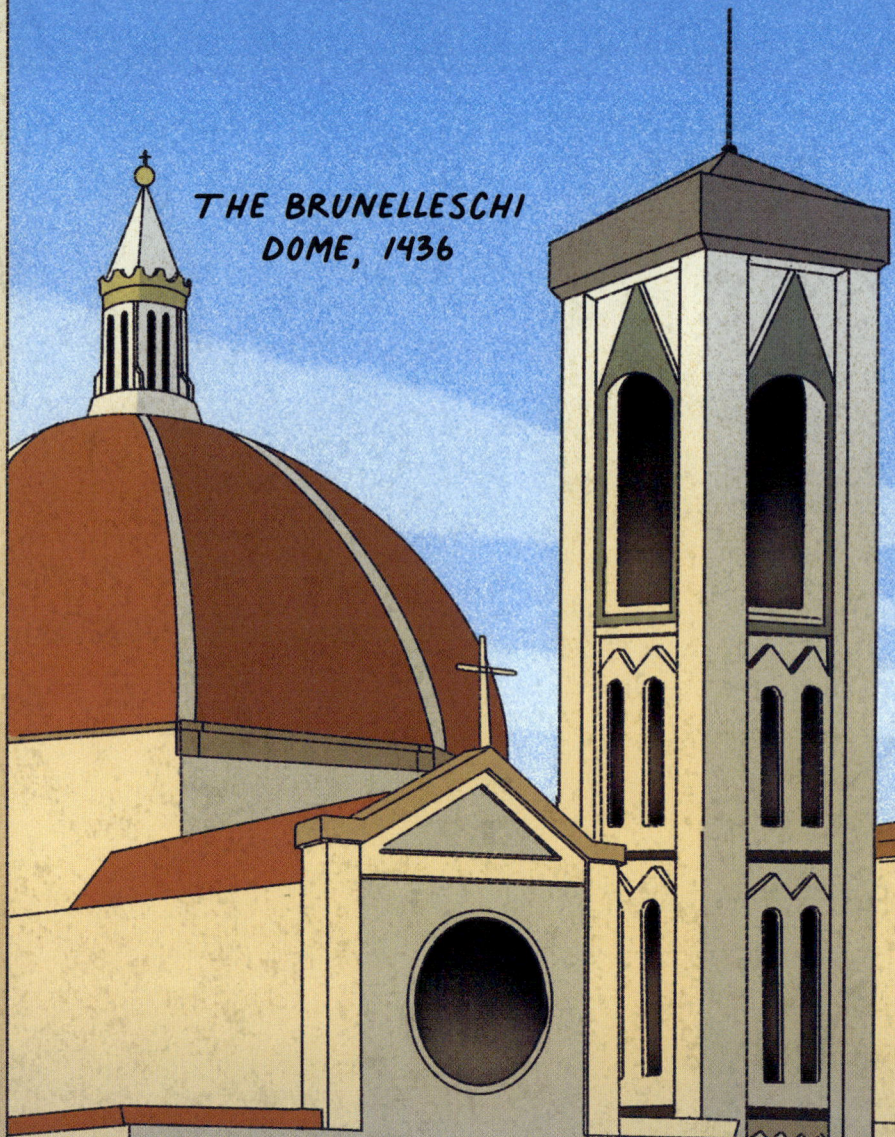

THE BRUNELLESCHI DOME, 1436

Architect *FILIPPO BRUNELLESCHI* went to see the ancient structures of Rome. He was so inspired that he built the *LARGEST BRICK DOME* in the world on the Cathedral of Florence. He used more than *FOUR MILLION BRICKS*!

*DONATELLO'S* sculpture of the prophet Habakkuk is often called *THE PUMPKIN* on account of his bald head! The figure looks so realistic, watching from high on the Cathedral bell tower.

Fra Angelico painted the walls of the monastery of San Marco. His **FRESCOES** (where the **COLOUR IS MIXED WITH PLASTER** and effectively painted into the wall) have inspired all those who see them.

## 1440
# FLORENCE, ITALY

### KEY ARTISTS: FRA ANGELICO AND DONATELLO

THE ARTISTS OF THE RENAISSANCE REDISCOVERED CLASSICAL IDEAS OF BEAUTY, HARMONY AND ORDER AND ADDED A NEW SENSE OF REALISM AND EMOTION TO CHANGE THE ART OF WESTERN EUROPE FOREVER. PAINTERS WORKED OUT HOW TO CREATE THE ILLUSION OF THREE DIMENSIONALITY ON A FLAT CANVAS, SCULPTORS BROUGHT STONE TO LIFE AND ARCHITECTS REACHED EXTRAORDINARY NEW FEATS OF ENGINEERING. THE CENTRE OF THE RENAISSANCE WAS FLORENCE. THE MEDICI FAMILY FINANCED MANY OF THE ARTISTS AND THEIR SUPPORT WAS CRUCIAL.

In **THE ANNUNCIATION**, Fra Angelico conveys the extraordinary **BEAUTY** in the wings of the angel and the leaves and flowers. The **GRACE** in this gentle work makes it something you could look at for hours – which the monks of the monastery in the 15th century would have done.

Craftsmen of the time looked after the children of the city and the **ARCHITECT BRUNELLESCHI** was asked to build an **ORPHANAGE**.

### THE ANNUNCIATION, 1450

The orphanage was decorated with colourful sculptures by **LUCA DELLA ROBBIA**, in another new invention in his use of enamelled terracotta.

23

The people of Benin WORSHIPPED SEVERAL GODS. According to their traditions, Osanobua created the world and his son, Olokun, became god of the waters, while his daughter, Obiemven, was goddess of farming and childbirth.

Although these plaques and sculptures works are often known by the collective name, 'THE BENIN BRONZES', they are mostly made from brass. They were carefully created using the complicated 'LOST-WAX' technique, where bronze is poured into a wax mould that is then melted away.

The wall begun by EWUARE THE GREAT to fortify the city finally stretched more than 10,000 kilometres. It is the second longest man-made structure after the Great Wall of China.

## 1550
# BENIN CITY, NIGERIA

KEY ARTISTS: THE GUILDS OF THE ROYAL COURTS OF THE KING

IN THE 16TH CENTURY, IN A COUNTRY WE NOW CALL NIGERIA IN WESTERN AFRICA, THERE ONCE STOOD THE MAGNIFICENT BENIN CITY. THIS WAS THE HEART OF THE SUCCESSFUL BENIN EMPIRE AND, SINCE THE 11TH CENTURY, IT HAD BEEN RULED OVER BY THE OBA (OR KING). IN 1504, OBA ESIGIE TOOK POWER AND CONTINUED TO BUILD THE AMAZING CITY THAT HAD BEEN LARGELY CONSTRUCTED BY HIS GRANDFATHER, EWUARE THE GREAT. THE PALACE WAS ENORMOUS, DECORATED WITH THOUSANDS OF BRASS PLAQUES LIKE THE ONE SHOWN HERE. AS ONLY THE OBA (OR KING) COULD OWN BRONZE, THIS WAS A HUGE DISPLAY OF WEALTH AND POWER.

In this sculpture, two men **GUARD THE PALACE WALLS** with their **DECORATED SHIELDS** and coral necklaces, headdresses and anklets showing their loyalty and pride. To each side, young boys hold fans and learn the ways of their community.

The people of **BENIN CITY** traded widely with their African neighbours as well as both European and Asian visitors, especially the Portuguese. **PEPPER** and **SPICES** were important as was **IVORY** and **CORAL**.

BENIN BRONZE PLAQUE, 1550

The city of Benin was arranged according to the jobs people did. **ARTISTS** worked in groups and the **BRASS-CASTERS** were the most important as they worked only for the king.

In the 19th century, the British wanted to take control of the **PALM OIL** and **RUBBER TRADE**. When the Oba refused, they launched the Punitive Expedition in 1897 as part of their colonial expansion. They destroyed the city, looted the artworks, bringing them to Britain. Today, Nigeria would like to see these **WORKS RETURNED HOME**.

SHIELDS HAVE LONG BEEN DECORATED TO SHOW THE VALUES OF A CIVILISATION AND TO STRENGTHEN THE SENSE OF PURPOSE AMONGST THE COMMUNITY. CAN YOU DESIGN A SHIELD THAT CELEBRATES THE IDEAS YOU THINK ARE IMPORTANT TODAY? REMEMBER, LIKE THE ARTISTS OF BENIN, YOU CAN INCLUDE SYMBOLIC ELEMENTS AND EXPERIMENT WITH PATTERN AND STRUCTURE TO MAKE YOUR WORK MORE EFFECTIVE...

The architect *MIMAR SINAN* had travelled much of the world with Suleyman's armies, but when his boss wanted the best mosque ever, the real competition was the glorious *HAGIA SOPHIA*, right on his doorstep.

## THE TUGHRA, 1550

The *'TUGHRA'* or *OFFICIAL STAMP OF THE RULER* is itself a beautiful work of art. Each section of the flower decorations between the blue letters is different.

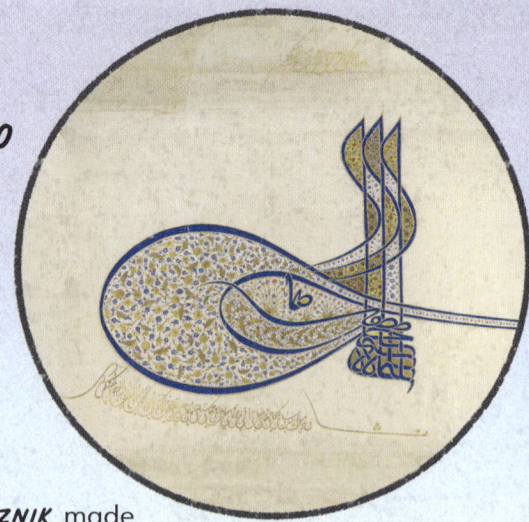

## HAGIA SOPHIA, 537 CE

Royal craftsmen from *IZNIK* made beautiful tiles, decorated with rich blues and reds... a uniquely Turkish artwork that drew *INSPIRATION* from the finest *PORCELAIN*.

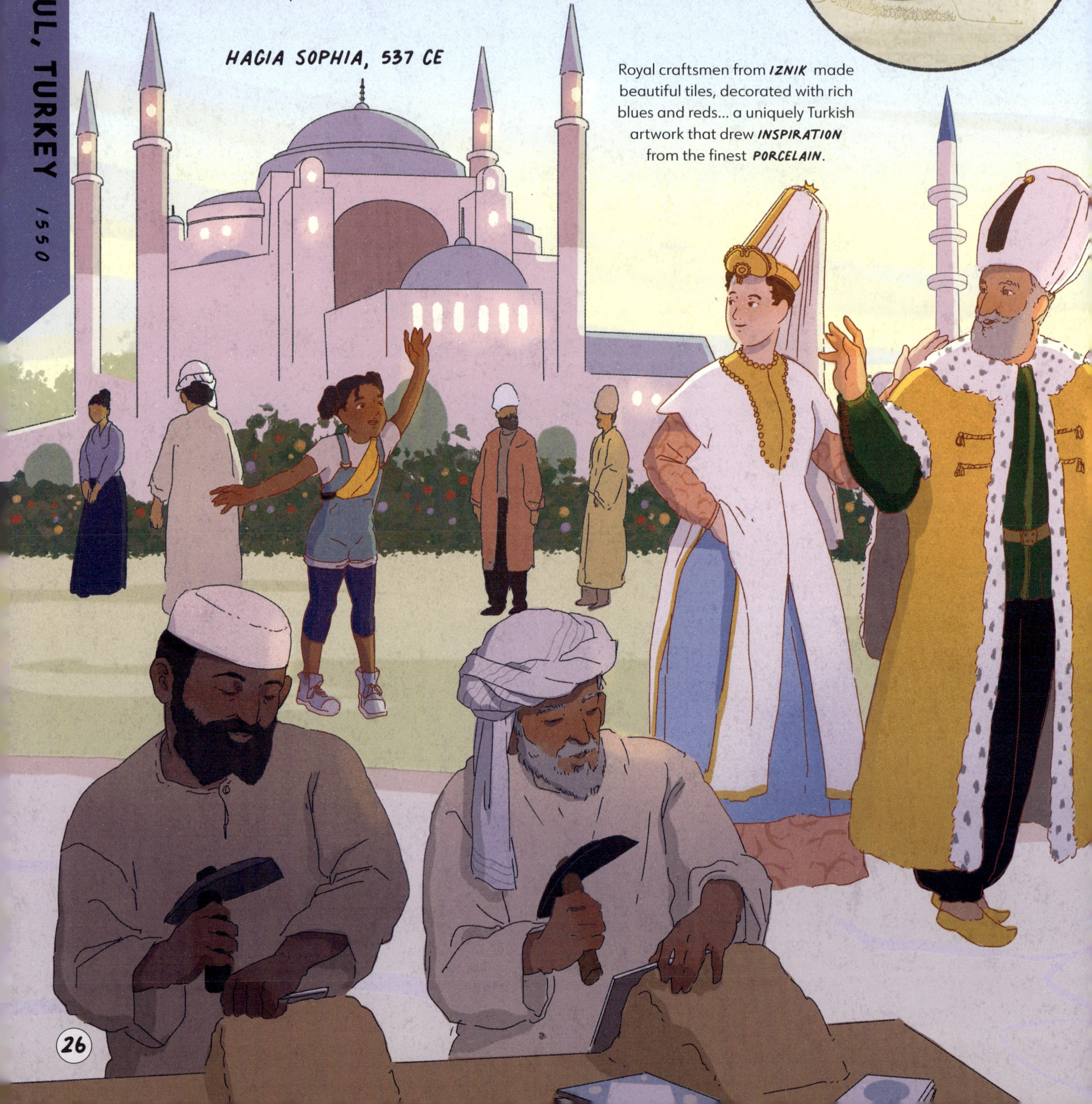

## THE SÜLEYMANIYE MOSQUE, 1550

The new Süleymaniye mosque had four pencil-thin *MINARETS*, with ten delicate balconies, a symbol of the tenth Emperor of the Ottoman Empire.

Black *MARBLE* from Baalbek in Lebanon, red granite from Egypt and *JEWELS* from all around the world decorate the building. The light-filled dome twinkles with treasures and *SUGGESTS THE HEAVENS*.

You can spot the face of Sultan Suleyman on the *US CAPITOL* building in Washington DC. The carving was made in recognition of his contribution to global law making.

Suleyman and his wife, Roxelana, or Sultan Hurrem, wanted to look after their people properly, so their *MOSQUE COMPLEX* also houses a school, university, hospital, soup kitchen, baths and even a hostel.

## 1550

# ISTANBUL, TURKEY

## KEY ARCHITECT: MIMAR SINAN

IN 1550, THE PRIZE FOR BIGGEST EMPIRE OF THE WORLD WENT TO SULTAN SULEYMAN AND HIS OTTOMAN EMPIRE. WITH A GLORIOUS CAPITAL CITY ON THE GOLDEN HORN, A CITY WHICH BRIDGED EAST AND WEST AND SPARKLED UNDER THE BRILLIANT SUNSHINE, HE SET ABOUT BUILDING A CULTURAL AND RELIGIOUS CAPITAL. SOME 25 MILLION PEOPLE LIVED IN OTTOMAN LANDS IN NORTH AFRICA, THE MIDDLE EAST AND EUROPE. KNOWN IN THE WEST AS SULTAN SULEYMAN THE MAGNIFICENT, AND TO HIS OWN PEOPLE AS SULEYMAN THE LAWGIVER, HE INTRODUCED A FAIR TAXATION SYSTEM AND REWARDED PEOPLE ON MERIT RATHER THAN THE LUCK OF THEIR BIRTH, AS WELL AS ALLOWING RELIGIOUS FREEDOM.

One of the most often discussed Spanish paintings is Velázquez's *LAS MENINAS* painted in 1656. It shows the young Princess Margaret Theresa, the first child of Philip and his second wife, Marianna, surrounded by members of the court in the Alcázar palace.

This painting is a *PAINTING OF PAINTING!* It shows a single moment in time and is riddled with mystery. What or who do you think the artist is painting on the big easel to the left? Find the small figures of the king and queen reflected in the mirror on the back wall. Everyone in this painting is looking in different directions – *WHAT COULD BE HAPPENING*?

Today, the work never moves from its home in the *PRADO MUSEUM* in Madrid, but you can look at it online in amazing detail using their high-resolution images of 14,000 megapixels.

THIS PAINTING CONTINUES TO FASCINATE MANY PAINTERS: IN 1957, ANOTHER FAMOUS SPANISH ARTIST, PABLO PICASSO, PAINTED 58 INTERPRETATIONS OF THIS WORK ALMOST EXACTLY 300 YEARS AFTER THE PAINT FIRST DRIED ON VELAZQUEZ'S CANVAS. CAN YOU MAKE YOUR OWN VERSION?

LAS MENINAS, 1656

His family lived at *EL ESCORIAL*, the enormous palace built by his grandfather, and at the *ALCÁZAR PALACE*. Philip asked his architect, Juan Gómez de Mora, to give this building a new appearance in the modern Baroque style.

Velázquez was only 24 when he became court painter to the king and during a long career he painted *MORE THAN 120 WORKS*, which give us a fantastic insight into how people lived in Spain at this time.

The king had *14 CHILDREN*, but most did not survive into adulthood, making Velázquez's paintings of them even more important for the king in these days *BEFORE PHOTOGRAPHY*.

In 1734, the *ALCÁZAR PALACE* was destroyed by an enormous *FIRE* on Christmas Eve. Many important *PAINTINGS WERE LOST*, but courtiers threw *Las Meninas* from a the window to safety.

## 1650
# MADRID, SPAIN

### KEY ARTIST: DIEGO VELÁZQUEZ

AFTER THE PERFECTION AND BEAUTY OF THE RENAISSANCE, ARTISTS WERE SET A NEW CHALLENGE: HOW TO BRING THEIR WORKS TO LIFE? FOR THE CATHOLIC CHURCH, THIS WAS REALLY IMPORTANT, SINCE THEY WERE WORRIED BY THE INCREASING NUMBER OF PEOPLE GOING TO PROTESTANT CHURCHES. THEY WANTED LIFELIKE ART TO SET THEM APART. FOR KINGS, DYNAMIC ART WAS A WAY TO SHOW THEIR POWER AND THE STYLE KNOWN AS 'BAROQUE' SPREAD ACROSS EUROPE AND OUT INTO THEIR COLONIES. IN SPAIN, THIS TIME WAS KNOWN AS THE 'GOLDEN AGE' OF CULTURE, WITH PAINTERS AND WRITERS CREATING WORKS WE STILL ENJOY TODAY. IN MADRID, KING PHILIP IV USED HIS COURT PAINTER, VELÁZQUEZ, TO PRESENT THE HOPES AND DREAMS OF HIS FAMILY.

1700

# AMSTERDAM, THE NETHERLANDS

## KEY ARTIST: RACHEL RUYSCH

AFTER THE DUTCH GAINED INDEPENDENCE FROM SPAIN IN THE 1648 TREATY OF MUNSTER, THEY CELEBRATED LIFE AND ALL ITS OPPORTUNITIES. IT LEAD TO A GROWTH IN EDUCATION, SCIENCE AND TRADE. THEY HAD TO THINK AGAIN ABOUT WHAT THEY WANTED TO PAINT. AS A RESULT, PAINTINGS SHOWING THEIR OWN LIVES, LANDS, SHIPS AT SEA, COLLECTIONS OF THINGS FROM ACROSS THE WORLD AND THEIR TREASURED FLOWERS BECAME A NEW FAVOURITE SUBJECT. ARTISTS SUCH AS REMBRANDT AND VERMEER PAINTED ENERGETICALLY AS AMSTERDAM FLOURISHED. RACHEL RUYSCH BECAME THE MOST SUCCESSFUL FLOWER PAINTER OF ALL TIME, EARNING AN INTERNATIONAL REPUTATION, AND EXTRAORDINARY CAREER.

News of Rachel's amazing work spread rapidly. Her works *BECAME SO POPULAR* that she became a court painter in Germany too.

Huge *DISCOVERIES* and *CHANGES* were being made. The invention of the microscope and the building of over *640 KILOMETRES OF CANALS* to connect cities made people curious about how life and nature worked.

30

It looks simple the first time you see it, but this painting actually contains *HIDDEN DETAILS*. In a time before the camera or cinema, people wanted pictures that you could *LOOK AT AGAIN AND AGAIN* and find something new.

Some people see the whole *STORY OF JESUS* here. The tree trunk as the cross, the stone as his tomb and the white and red flowers as symbols of the bread and blood of communion. Or the *WHITE, BLACK* and *RED* colours might be a reminder of *BIRTH, LIFE* and *DEATH*.

Some people simply enjoy the *AMAZING DETAIL* of all the different flowers apparently blooming at the same time. Some are in full flower and some still in bud. That tree trunk is wonderfully knarly!

There are many *INSECTS* hiding in the picture, eating the plants. Rachel knew they were important for spreading their seeds and creating *NEW LIFE*.

FLOWERS IN A TREE, 1700

Rachel's *FATHER* was a *DOCTOR* and *BOTANIST*. As a young girl, she helped him with his *EXPERIMENTS* at conserving plants and insects. This sharpened her interest and knowledge in the *NATURAL WORLD*.

# LONDON, BRITAIN

## KEY ARTIST: GEORGE STUBBS

IN 18TH-CENTURY BRITAIN, BEFORE THE INVENTION OF THE TRAIN, HORSEPOWER WAS THE TRUE ENGINE OF THE COUNTRY. HORSES WERE KEY FOR TRANSPORT, AGRICULTURE, WAR AND MINING AS WELL AS FOR LEISURE, RACING AND AS A MARK OF STATUS. AT THIS TIME, THE NEOCLASSICAL STYLE WAS SPREADING ACROSS EUROPE. CALM GRANDEUR AND HEROIC DEPICTIONS WERE HUGELY POPULAR, STRONGLY INFLUENCED BY THE IDEALS AND EMPIRES OF CLASSICAL GREEK AND ROME. GEORGE STUBBS' EPIC PAINTING 'WHISTLEJACKET' IS CERTAINLY GRAND AND A PERFECT EXAMPLE OF NEOCLASSICAL STYLE.

George Stubbs was born in Liverpool where his father was a leather worker. He moved to York to *STUDY ANATOMY* at the newly built York County Hospital before deciding to concentrate on the muscles and body of horses.

Charles Wentworth-Watson, Marquess of Rockingham, commissioned this painting of his favourite horse. He had enjoyed a privileged position at the court of *KING GEORGE II,* but fell out of favour in 1760. Some think that the painting was originally *INTENDED TO SHOW THE KING RIDING* Whistlejacket.

WHISTLEJACKET, 1762

Whistlejacket was *BEATEN* in a race *ONLY FOUR TIMES* in his career, but was notorious for being temperamental and difficult to manage.

George Stubbs was famous as a great painter of animals. He made the **FIRST PAINTINGS** of the *KANGAROO* and *DINGO* seen in Britain.

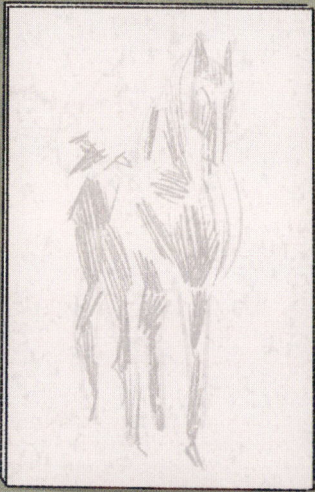

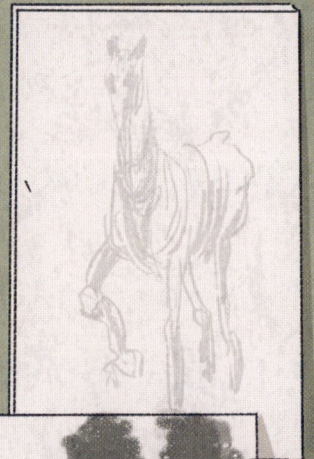

EYE OF THE NEEDLE, 1760

*CHARLES WENTWORTH-WATSON* adored horses. He once claimed that he could ride a coach and horses through the 'eye of the needle' and so he built an enormous 'eye of the needle' stone arch at his home to win his bet!

It was designed in the *NEOCLASSICAL* style by John Carr, an architect who also built a hospital, prison and racecourse in Yorkshire – as well as becoming Lord Mayor of the city of York.

## 1830

# EDO, JAPAN

### KEY ARTIST: KATSUSHIKA HOKUSAI

IN AN ISLAND COUNTRY SURROUNDED BY THE SEA AND FULL OF WONDERFUL MOUNTAINS, FORESTS AND WATER, ONE OF THE WORLD'S MOST FAMOUS ARTISTS WAS BORN IN 1760. KATSUSHIKA HOKUSAI WAS BORN IN EDO (NOW TOKYO) AND HE JOINED A LONG TRADITION OF EXQUISITE ART, DEEP THINKERS AND STRONG CULTURE IN JAPAN. DURING HIS LONG LIFE, HE WAS A HUGELY SUCCESSFUL PAINTER, PRINT-MAKER AND DESIGNER BUT HE NEVER BECAME WEALTHY. HIS WORKS TELL AMAZING STORIES OF THE POWER OF NATURE AS WELL AS ITS EXTRAORDINARY BEAUTY.

The man we now call KATSUSHIKA HOKUSAI CHANGED HIS NAME many times. His first name, Katsushika, is the part of the town in which he grew up. Later in life he called himself Gakyō Rōjin 'OLD MAN MAD ABOUT ART'.

According to legend, Katsushika Hokusai once dipped his CHICKEN'S FEET in RED PAINT and then chased it across the paper. He told the watching crowd that it was a landscape of a river with RED LEAVES floating on it!

This wave in the image is a *TSUNAMI*. The word tsunami means *'HARBOUR WAVE'*. Most tsunamis are triggered by earthquakes or volcanoes erupting under the sea. As Japan lies on several tectonic plates, these huge waves are a regular feature of life in Japan, both when Katsushika Hokusai was alive and today.

## THE GREAT WAVE, 1830

The Great Wave has been **REPRODUCED MILLIONS OF TIMES** on everything from surf boards and bank notes to T-shirts and house walls. It was the **FIRST WORK OF ART** to have **ITS OWN EMOJI**!

In the background, you can see **MOUNT FUJI**. This sacred mountain is almost 4,000 metres high. Katsushika Hokusai painted it often, in every season and weather. He began making art when he was just six years old, and in his lifetime he made **30,000 ARTWORKS**.

Art like this from Japan is known as **'UKIYO-E'** which means **PICTURES OF THE FLOATING WORLD**. It's a reminder to make the most of every day and comes from the **BUDDHIST RELIGION** that Katsushika Hokusai followed and loved.

The image was originally made as a **PRINT** and sold for the **PRICE OF A BOWL OF NOODLES**. Art was a treat for everyone to enjoy, **NOT AN EXPENSIVE LUXURY** reserved only for the elite.

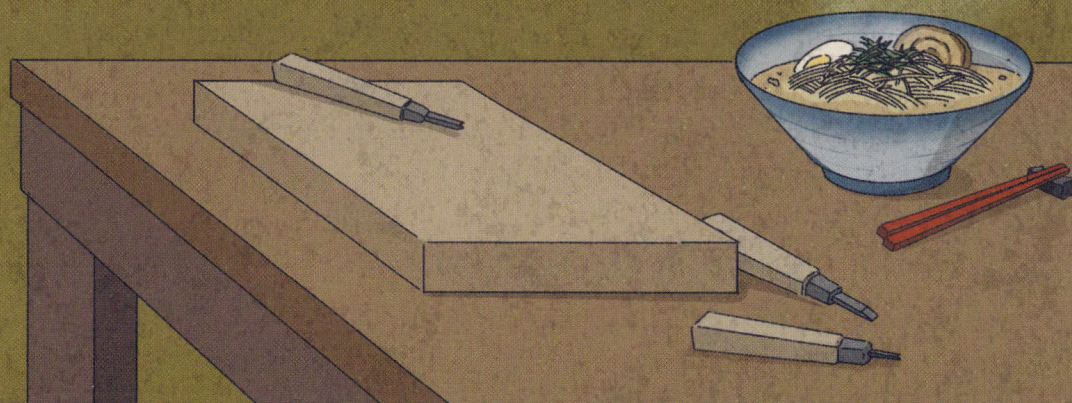

GUSTAV MAHLER   ALBAN BERG   JOSEPH OLBRICH

**JOSEPH OLBRICH** built the new exhibition space called the **SECESSION BUILDING**. When its golden dome was put in place, critics called it *'THE GOLDEN CABBAGE'*!

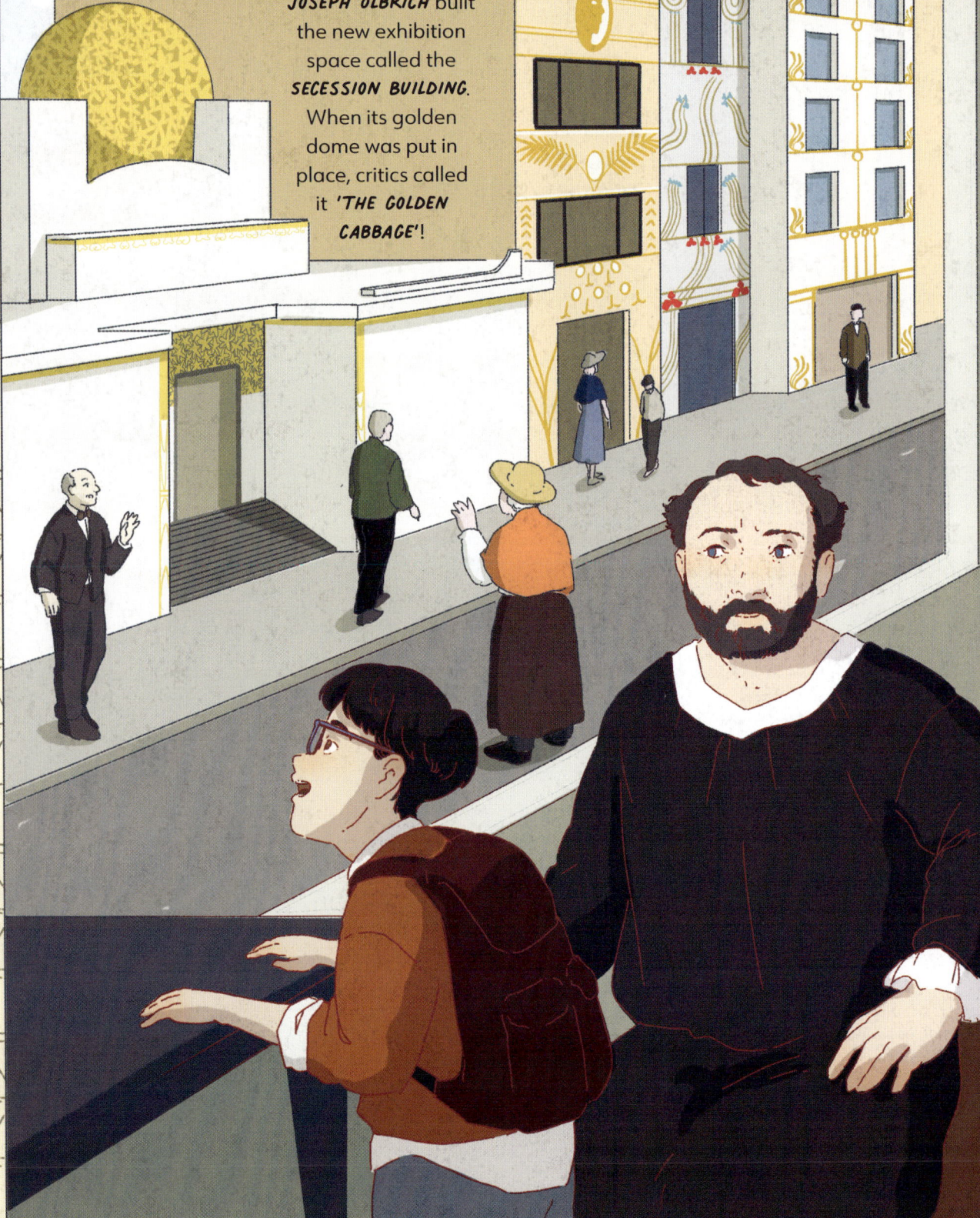

**ARCHITECT** Joseph Olbrich worked with artists but also **COMPOSERS**. He was inspired by composers such as Alban Berg and Gustav Mahler, who composed music which played at the opening of the **SECESSION BUILDING**.

Vienna was a place for ideas to blossom. Many artists of the time included **FLOWERS** in their work for this reason. They are on the **OUTSIDE OF BUILDINGS** like the Majolica House designed by Otto Wagner and Alois Ludwig.

# VIENNA, AUSTRIA

## KEY ARTIST: GUSTAV KLIMT

AS THE NEW 20TH CENTURY LOOMED, ARTISTS IN VIENNA WANTED TO CHANGE THE WAY ART AND BUILDINGS LOOKED AND THE WAY THAT MUSIC SOUNDED. THESE NEW ARTISTS CALLED THEMSELVES THE VIENNA SECESSION AND THEY WERE HEADED BY PAINTER GUSTAV KLIMT. SECESSION MEANT 'TO BREAK AWAY'. THEY BUILT A NEW ART SPACE IN THE CITY. INFLUENCED BY THE RECENT INDUSTRIAL GROWTH, ARRIVALS OF JAPANESE ARTWORKS IN EUROPE AND THE IMPORTANCE OF A HAND-MADE APPROACH, THESE ARTISTS WANTED TO CREATE A NEW GLOWING VISION OF BEAUTY. THEY SHARED THEIR IDEAS IN A MAGAZINE THEY MADE CALLED 'VER SACRUM', MEANING SACRED SPRING.

Emilie Flöge, the woman in *THE KISS*, was a fashion designer and collector of *JAPANESE TEXTILES*. We can see her interests reflected in the patterns in her clothing. This is very different from painting people *REALISTICALLY*, which was more common at the time.

One of the most famous paintings from this era is *THE KISS* by Gustav Klimt. It shows him and the love of his life, Emilie Flöge. Many admire it for the *BEAUTIFUL PATTERNS* and the *SENSITIVE* way it shows long-lasting affection.

The figures are shown against a dark gold background, which suggests *THEY COULD BE ANYWHERE* at any time. The gold suggests the idea of spiritual *DIVINE POWER* that Klimt had seen in golden *BYZANTINE MOSAICS* on his travels in Italy.

Notice how all the *PATTERNS* on the man's clothes are *SQUARES AND RECTANGLES*, while those on the woman's are more curvy: *CIRCLES AND OVALS*.

**THE KISS, 1908**

There is **NOT MUCH DETAIL** in this painting. The hills echo the **CURVES** and colour of the horse. The **YELLOW** is calming, but Franz thought that **RED** was a dangerous colour. Notice how the horse stamps on that part.

**MUNICH, GERMANY** *1910*

Franz believed that animals could show a **PURE LIFE** and an **HONEST SPIRIT**. His painting *Blue Horse 1* is much more simple than Stubb's rearing *Whistlejacket* on page 32. It's **NOT REALISTIC**, but in its humble pose and primary colours, it conveys **CALM**, **HOPE** and **HARMONY**.

The group looked **ALL OVER THE WORLD** for ideas on how to shape the new art. They liked the simplicity and power of **AFRICAN AND SOUTH PACIFIC ART**, the pure colour in **JAPANESE ART** and the honest spirit in **CHILDREN'S ART**.

Music was important to the group, too. Wassily called many of his works '**COMPOSITIONS**' or '**HARMONIES**'. These were some of the first examples of **ABSTRACT ART**. If you could enjoy music without lyrics, then you could also enjoy art without a story. **COLOUR** and **SHAPE** became the most important tools.

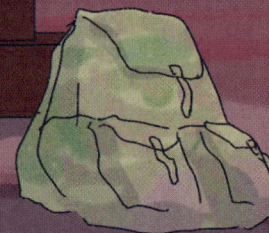

# 1910
# MUNICH, GERMANY

## KEY ARTIST: FRANZ MARC

AFTER THE INVENTION OF THE CAMERA, ARTISTS WANTED MORE FROM THEIR ART THAN REALISTIC COPIES OF THINGS. A GROUP OF GERMAN AND RUSSIAN ARTISTS IN MUNICH WANTED ART TO BE ABOUT EXPRESSION — OR FEELINGS. REVOLUTIONS IN RUSSIA AND CHINA, HEAVY INDUSTRIALISATION ACROSS EUROPE AND THE RECENT ASSASSINATION OF THE AMERICAN PRESIDENT HINTED AT A DISTURBING WORLD. THEY WANTED ART TO FIND ITS SPIRITUAL PLACE AWAY FROM SUCH TROUBLES. THEY CALLED THEMSELVES THE BLUE RIDER GROUP AND AS WELL AS THEIR MANY PAINTINGS, THEY CREATED THE 'BLUE RIDER JOURNAL' AND COLLECTED NEW ARTWORKS, INCLUDING THOSE MADE BY CHILDREN.

*BLUE* has always been important in art. It was once the most expensive pigment, made from *LAPIS LAZULI* stone imported from Afghanistan. It was used to identify Mary, the mother of Jesus, in much Christian art.

*FRANZ MARC, GABRIELE MÜNTER* and their Russian friend, *WASSILY KANDINSKY*, were the founders of the group. They chose the name *'THE BLUE RIDER'* because Franz loved horses, Wassily loved riders, and they all loved the colour blue.

Franz and his friends were worried that people were being damaged by *MODERNISATION* and money worries. They wanted to make art that would be *GOOD FOR THE SOUL*.

Vladimir Tatlin designed a *MONUMENT TO THE REVOLUTION* which became known as *TATLIN'S TOWER*. If it had been built, it would have been twice as tall as the Eiffel Tower. He imagined that the different floors would rotate, so that those inside would see everything around them clearly.

Vladimir, Varvara and Aleksandra were *CONSTRUCTIVISTS*. This group of artists brought *ALL PARTS OF MODERN LIFE* into their work. They decorated streets, town squares and even the sides of trains to get their message to as many people as possible.

TATLIN'S TOWER, 1919—20

Constructivists in Moscow were among the first artists to work across *FASHION*, *PHOTOGRAPHY*, *ADVERTISING* and *ARCHITECTURE*.

In Russia, the *THEATRE* had always been an important setting for new art and many of these new artists created *SETS* and *COSTUMES*. Sergei Diaghilev's *BALLETS* with designs by Natalia Goncharova brought them both worldwide fame.

Vladimir imagined that the tower would *BROADCAST NEWS* and even have an open-air screen from which to *BEAM MESSAGES ON TO THE CLOUDS*! All this, long before the invention of the television.

40

# MOSCOW, RUSSIA

## KEY ARTISTS: VLADIMIR TATLIN AND ALEKSANDRA EXTER

BOTH ART AND SOCIETY WERE SHAKEN TO THE CORE IN RUSSIA IN THE EARLY 20TH CENTURY. THE OCTOBER REVOLUTION OF 1917 SAW THE END OF THE LONG RULE OF THE TSARS AND THE ARRIVAL OF COMMUNISM UNDER LENIN. IN ART TOO, THE CITY WAS A MELTING POT OF IDEAS AS ARTISTS EXPERIMENTED WITH WAYS TO INVOLVE EVERYONE IN THEIR NEW MODERN VISION. PAINTERS OF 'THE JACK OF DIAMONDS' GROUP WERE KNOWN FOR THEIR RADICAL AND COLOURFUL IDEAS, WHILE THOSE OF THE CONSTRUCTIVIST GROUP MADE ABSTRACT AND GEOMETRIC WORK.

AELITA COSTUME DESIGN, 1920

Influenced by the rapid **MODERNISATION** of Russia, **ALEKSANDRA EXTER** designed this **COSTUME** for the sci-fi film *Aelita* about a man falling in love with the Queen of Mars.

**VARVARA STEPANOVA** explored the future of clothing design as **FUNCTIONAL** and practical, rather than showing ideas of **CLASS** or **GENDER**.

41

THIS PAINTING on Frida's easel is called SELF PORTRAIT WITH THORN NECKLACE AND HUMMINGBIRD. She explores some of her most important ideas in it. She gazes straight at us, unafraid – challenging us to be fierce too!

You can spot LOTS OF DIFFERENT STORIES in this painting: the HUMMINGBIRD is a symbol of Huitzilopochtli, the Aztec God of War. The THORNS might make you think of the crown worn by Jesus on the cross. Do you think the black MONKEY and black CAT are spooky or friendly?

The BACKGROUND OF LEAVES make the top half of the painting much lighter than the bottom. Maybe the shimmering butterflies, calm green and bright sky might be a way of showing her determination to LOOK FOR THE LIGHT, despite all the pain in her life?

Frida's favourite place was her childhood home, THE BLUE HOUSE. The walls were painted bright blue and it was filled it with objects that were precious to her. The house now belongs to the city and is a popular place to visit.

SELF PORTRAIT WITH THORN NECKLACE AND HUMMINGBIRD, 1940

FRIDA'S PAINTINGS are much more famous today than they were during her own lifetime. She is an inspiration not just for her painting but also for her CAMPAIGNING for the RIGHTS OF WOMEN and MARGINALISED PEOPLES.

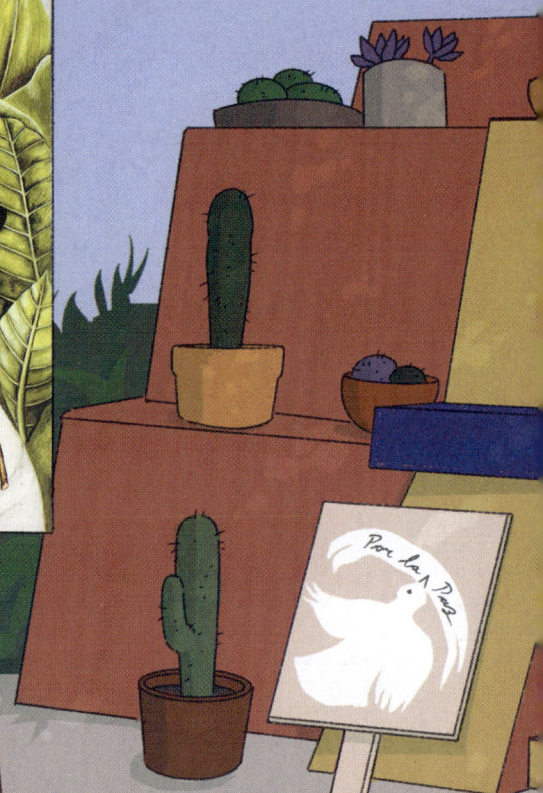

## 1940

# COYOÁCAN, MEXICO

### KEY ARTIST: FRIDA KAHLO

IN A DISTRICT OF MEXICO CITY, FRIDA KAHLO WAS BORN TO A GERMAN REFUGEE FATHER AND MEXICAN MOTHER. FRIDA DREAMT OF CHANGING THE WORLD. FIRST, SHE THOUGHT OF BECOMING A DOCTOR, BUT A TERRIBLE BUS CRASH MEANT SHE SPENT A LOT OF TIME RECUPERATING IN BED. SHE CAME UP WITH A NEW WAY TO SHARE HER DREAMS - PAINTING! IT GAVE HER A WAY TO REACH AN AUDIENCE BEYOND HER BED. FRIDA WANTED TO SHARE IMPORTANT IDEAS ABOUT HER COUNTRY AND THE COMMUNITY SHE WANTED TO BE PART OF. SHE PAINTED MANY SMALL SELF-PORTRAITS THROUGH WHICH WE CAN EXPLORE HER IDEAS. HER FATHER HELPED BY RIGGING UP A MIRROR AND EASEL SO SHE COULD EVEN WORK LYING DOWN.

Frida's paintings were small, but other artists in Mexico were famous for *HUGE MURALS* in public places which could be seen by everyone. *DIEGO RIVERA*, *DAVID SIQUEIROS* and *JOSÉ CLEMENTE OROZCO* all depicted the history of their country in their own styles, and together they are known as *'THE BIG THREE'*.

*FRIDA WAS BORN IN 1907*, but she liked to tell everyone that her birthday was actually in 1910, the year the Mexican Revolution began. She was passionate about the right for land, liberty and justice for all Mexicans.

Lots of her paintings focus on her *NATIONAL IDENTITY* and many of her portraits refer to the folk traditions and rituals of her *HOMELAND* from the days before it was *COLONISED BY SPAIN*.

Frida married *DIEGO RIVERA*, Mexico's most famous artist at the time. They had a fiery relationship, but *INSPIRED EACH OTHER* artistically and politically.

In this painting, Ibrahim El-Salahi explores the *NOISES OF HIS CHILDHOOD*. He called it *REBORN SOUNDS OF CHILDHOOD DREAMS* and plays with the ideas that all our childhoods are shaped by both *GOOD AND SCARY MEMORIES*.

The painting does not use many colours. For Ibrahim, this was a way of connecting with the *COLOURS OF THE EARTH* of Sudan, especially with the striking *DESERT LANDSCAPE*.

*IN THIS PICTURE,* the shapes that once marked out words in calligraphy have now turned into *STRANGE ANIMALS, PEOPLE AND PLANTS*. The figures merge together reminding us that our *MEMORIES CONSTANTLY SHIFT* and take different shapes too. Can you draw the sounds of your childhood memories?

REBORN SOUNDS OF CHILDHOOD DREAMS, 1960

*IN THIS PICTURE,* Ibrahim takes inspiration from *ARABIC CALLIGRAPHY*. Moving away from the meanings of the letters and words to the actual shapes themselves. The idea was called *'HURUFIYYAH'* from the Arabic word meaning letter.

## 1960

# KHARTOUM, SUDAN

### KEY ARTIST: IBRAHIM EL-SALAHI

SUDAN GAINED INDEPENDENCE FROM BRITAIN IN 1956 AND IN THE SAME YEAR CREATED THE UNIVERSITY OF KHARTOUM IN ITS CAPITAL CITY. ARTISTS HERE WERE KEEN TO EXPLORE THEIR UNIQUE HERITAGE AND TO BRING TOGETHER THEIR AFRICAN, ISLAMIC AND ARABIC IDENTITIES. MANY WANTED TO EXPRESS THE HOPES OF THEIR NEW, FREE NATION. ONCE THE HOME OF THE PHARAOHS, AND LATER THE NUBIAN KINGDOM OF KUSH, THERE WAS AN EXTRAORDINARY HISTORY AND CULTURE TO EXPLORE. THESE ARTISTS WERE ALSO PART OF A MUCH LARGER DISCUSSION ABOUT INDEPENDENCE CALLED THE PAN-AFRICAN MOVEMENT AS NEW COUNTRIES EMERGED FROM COLONIAL RULE ALL OVER THE CONTINENT.

Members of the new *KHARTOUM SCHOOL* group included *ARTISTS, POETS* and *WRITERS* too: all excited to share and shape the newly independent country.

*OSMAN* even designed the first *BANK NOTES* for the new country in 1956 and welcomed many artists and thinkers to his studio to share their ideas.

Many young Sudanese artists were *INSPIRED* by the work of *OSMAN WAQIALLA* who explored the intricate and complicated shapes of *ARABIC CALLIGRAPHY* as a system of sweeping lines and light dark contrasts.

*OSMAN* taught Ibrahim El-Salahi, Ahmed Shibrain and Kamal Ishag who continued his mission, working together to make a *NEW MODERNIST ART FOR SUDAN* that became known as *THE KHARTOUM SCHOOL*.

Ibrahim was *BORN IN OMDURMAN* on the banks of the White Nile river. The city is across the water from Khartoum and is one of the *HOTTEST CITIES ON EARTH*. His father was in charge of a Quaranic school so learning *ISLAMIC CALLIGRAPHY* was an important part of his childhood even before he was taught y Osman Waqialla.

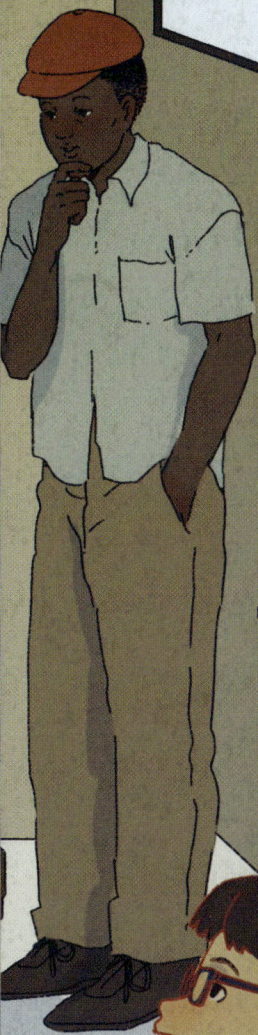

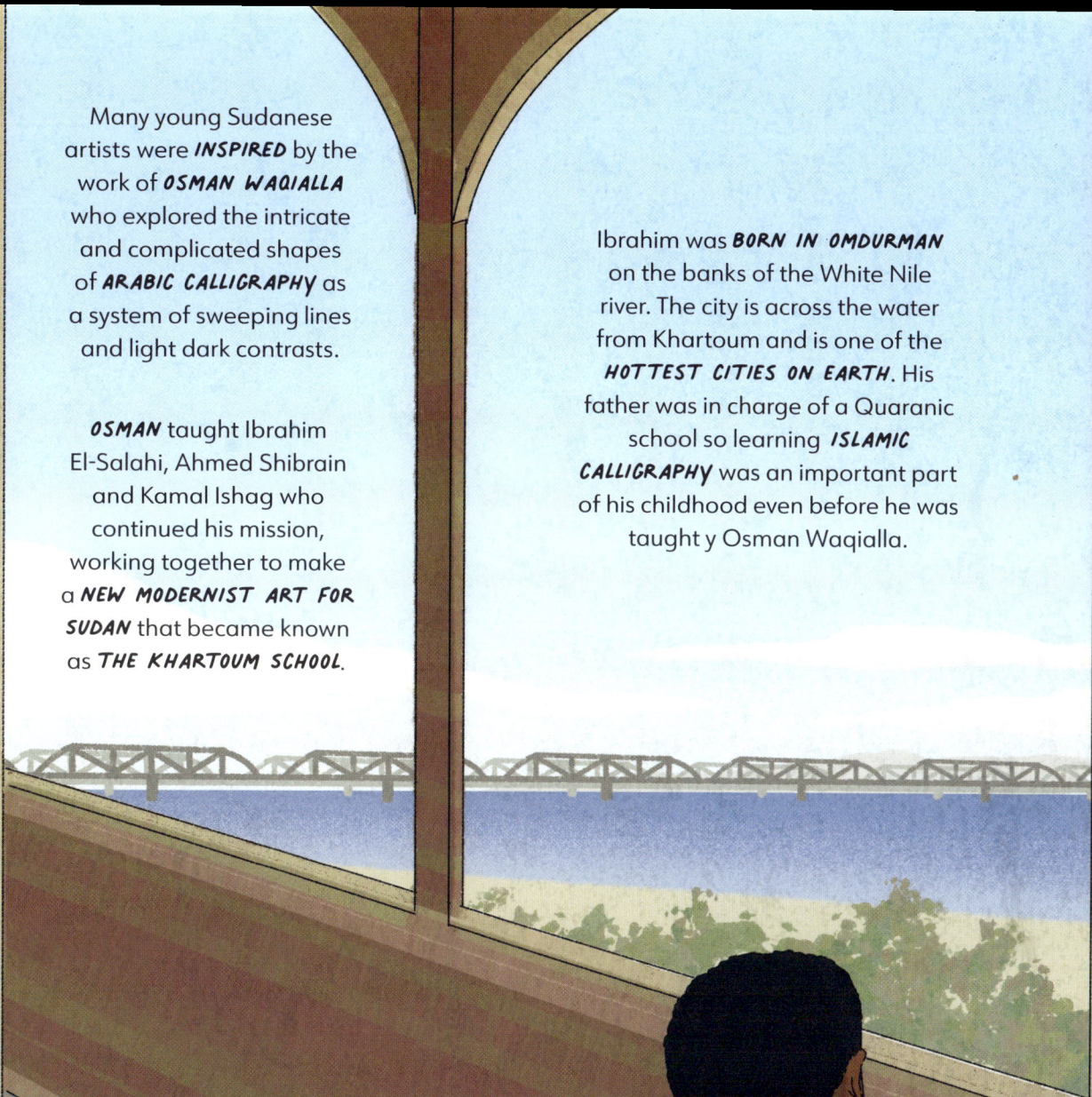

When she found an abandoned *WINDOW FRAME* next to Big Bear Lake in California, Betye Saar wanted to give it new life as a piece of art. Rather than looking through the window, she wants us to look into it. It's like a *DIARY* of *HER MEMORIES*.

*AS A CHILD*, Betye had been inspired by the extraordinary *WATTS TOWERS* or *NUESTRO PUEBLO* (which means 'our town' in Spanish) built by Sabato Rodia. These huge structures were decorated with broken things.

## BLACK GIRL'S WINDOW, 1969

The *TOP ROW* makes us think of looking up at the *STARS* and the *MOON* and *DREAMING* about the bigger world out there.

In the *MIDDLE ROW*, two children dance to remind her of her own parents. In the middle, the skeleton suggests the *LOSS OF HER FATHER* when she was little. Perhaps the brain on the right is to remind us that ideas can help make the world a fairer place.

In the *BOTTOM PANE*, the artist looks directly at us. Shiny bit of glass makes her eyes seem to move and *WE BECOME THE WATCHED* rather than the watcher. Pressing her hands up against the glass, *SHE IS ASKING US TO THINK* about how we behave.

HAVE A GO AT MAKING YOUR OWN ART DIARY, LIKE BETYE SAAR. WHAT THINGS COULD YOU BRING TOGETHER TO SYMBOLISE MEMORIES AND IDEAS THAT ARE SPECIAL TO YOU?

# 1970
# LOS ANGELES, USA

## KEY ARTIST: BETYE SAAR

THE 1960S WAS A TIME OF HUGE CHANGE IN THE USA. THE SHOCKING ASSASSINATION OF THE HUMAN RIGHTS ACTIVIST MALCOLM X AND MARTIN LUTHER KING JUNIOR DURING THIS DECADE FUELLED THE CIVIL RIGHTS MOVEMENT AND THE BLACK ARTS MOVEMENT TO SHARE THEIR VOICES AND STORIES. FOR ARTIST BETYE SAAR WORKING IN CALIFORNIA, USA, THE EFFORTS TO CREATE BETTER OPPORTUNITIES PARTICULARLY FOR WOMEN AND BLACK PEOPLE, WERE HUGELY IMPORTANT. BETYE'S 'ASSEMBLAGE' ARTWORKS USE BOTH PRINTING AND FOUND OBJECTS TO CREATE A VISION OF NEW HOPE AND DREAMS. SAAR ENJOYED ASSEMBLING ARTWORKS FROM ABANDONED THINGS LONG BEFORE MANY OF US HAD THOUGHT ABOUT RECYCLING AND UPCYCLING. SHE WAS RIGHT: USING SOMETHING OLD IN A NEW WAY CAN ADD LAYERS OF MEANING AND MAKE THE NEW PIECE REALLY INTERESTING TO LOOK AT.

NUESTRO PUEBLO

In 1965, this part of Los Angeles saw *RIOTS* and unrest after a young black man was killed by the police. This shaped Betye's ideas as well as those of another famous storyteller at the time: the writer *MAYA ANGELOU*.

47

1978

# MANITOULIN ISLAND, CANADA

*ARTIST: DAPHNE ODJIG*

DAPHNE ODJIG WAS BORN IN 1919 IN WIIKWEMKOONG ON MANITOULIN ISLAND — THE LARGEST FRESHWATER ISLAND IN THE WORLD AND AN UNCEDED INDIAN RESERVE. AT 13, SHE HAD TO GIVE UP SCHOOL BECAUSE SHE WAS TOO UNWELL, BUT SHE WOULD GO ON TO BECOME THE GREATEST FIRST NATION ARTIST CANADA HAS EVER KNOWN. HER ENORMOUS WORK 'THE INDIAN IN TRANSITION' TELLS THE STORY OF ABORIGINAL PEOPLE OVER HUNDREDS OF YEARS. THIS PAINTING IS A TREASURE HUNT. LOOK CAREFULLY AND SEE IF YOU CAN UNDERSTAND THE STORIES SHE TELLS WITH PICTURES.

*THE INDIAN IN TRANSITION, 1978*

*THE STORY BEGINS* on the left. Beneath the protection of the *MYTHICAL THUNDERBIRD,* the people start off as a tight community, telling stories and singing songs, accompanied by the drum.

*IN THE MIDDLE,* the Europeans arrive – can you find the ship with its crew of white sailors in the middle? The captain waves a flag above his head, excited to claim these lands. The indigenous people look on, worried.

The character with a white face who appears behind the sailors **REPRESENTS CHRISTIANITY**. She holds a book, builds a church and draws the people towards her with bible stories. The people around her have no faces. Odjig is showing the way that Christian teaching tried to **TAKE AWAY INDIGENOUS PEOPLE'S VOICES AND IDENTITIES**.

Daphne Odjig is known as the **'GRANDMOTHER OF ABORIGINAL PAINTING'**. Inspired by the spirit and stories of her people, she set up the first gallery for Aboriginal art in Winnipeg in 1972.

**THE STORY ENDS** on the right. The people re-emerge and are **PROTECTED** by the **THUNDERBIRD**. At his heart, the eye (and egg) shines brightly because a **NEW GENERATION** is coming.

Beneath the boat, **THE DRUMS HAVE BROKEN**, just like the hearts of the indigenous people whose land is being stolen.

Next, the aboriginal people break away. Can you find the figure on the right who holds **A NEW DRUM**? Perhaps the bird on her drum is a **PHOENIX**, rising from the ashes?

Odjig was inspired by **PABLO PICASSO**. He made the painting **GUERNICA** to support his people. In his case, he was horrified by the bombing of the Basque town in Spain in World War II. Both artists used a **LARGE CANVAS** to tell a powerful story from **LEFT TO RIGHT**.

# 1992

# GHANA

## KEY ARTIST: EL ANATSUI

NOW THAT PEOPLE COULD TRAVEL ANYWHERE, MANY ARTISTS DIDN'T FEEL THE MOST IMPORTANT THING TO PAINT WAS THEIR OWN PLACE AND TIME. IN AN ERA OF INCREASING CONCERN ABOUT CLIMATE CHANGE AND ENVIRONMENTAL DESTRUCTION, MANY ARTISTS ACROSS THE WORLD HAVE MADE WORKS WHICH HELP TO MOTIVATE CHANGE IN US ALL. EL ANATSUI IS POSSIBLY THE MOST IMPORTANT GHANIAN ARTIST OF ALL TIME. HE MAKES WORK THAT EXPLORES THE DESTRUCTION OF TREES. BORN IN ACCRA (NOW GHANA), EL ANATSUI INHERITED A TRADITION OF TEXTILES AND STORYTELLING. HE USES MANY DIFFERENT MATERIALS TO TELL STORIES THAT HARNESS HIS WEST AFRICAN ROOTS WITH THE ISSUES OF OUR WHOLE WORLD TODAY. HE IS A SCULPTOR WHO WEAVES OLD AND NEW TO MAKE VERY SPECIAL ART.

The height of this twisting column might remind you of both a *GROWING TREE* and the scary idea of something *THREATENING* you from above.

El Anatsui adopted the phrase *SANKOFA* to describe his movement. It is a Ghanaian term meaning 'go back and pick', and refers to the process of *RECLAIMING ONE'S ROOTS* in the act of making art. The backward-facing sankofa bird *SYMBOLISES* the wisdom of *LEARNING FROM THE PAST*.

This work, called Erosion was made for the *EARTH SUMMIT* in Brazil in 1992. The organisers of that event wanted to draw attention to the shocking devastation of the *AMAZON RAINFOREST*.

El Anatsui is concerned about disappearing languages and cultures in his home region. The motifs you can see are *ADINKRA SYMBOLS* from Ghana's ancient *AKAN PEOPLE* to suggest all the wisdom and connections between people being lost.

The *SCRAPS* of wood at the bottom of the piece are there to remind us of damage done – by *loggers* and *politicians*.

*LOOK AROUND YOUR HOUSE – HOW COULD YOU WEAVE STORIES FROM THINGS THAT YOU ALREADY HAVE?*

EROSION, 1992

Carved from Pau Marfim tropical wood, with a *CHAINSAW AND A BLOW TORCH*, El Anatsui used the *SAME TOOLS* to shape the wood that also *DESTROY THE RAINFORESTS*.

## 1994
# UTOPIA, AUSTRALIA

### KEY ARTIST: EMILY KAME KNGWARREYE

EMILY KAME KNGWARREYE WAS ONE OF AUSTRALIA'S MOST SIGNIFICANT CONTEMPORATY ARTISTS AS WELL AS A RESPECTED SENIOR ANMATYERRE WOMAN. SHE GREW UP LEARNING EVERYTHING ABOUT HER TREASURED LAND ALHALKERE. SHE LEARNED THE STORIES, SONGS, CEREMONIES AND RESPONISIBLITIES THAT HAD BEEN PASSED DOWN FROM GENERATION TO GENERATION AND THESE INFLUENCES WERE A LIVING PART OF HER ARTWORK. TO EMILY, THE SPECIAL BLEND OF PLACE AND COMMUNITY AND HISTORY WAS IMPORTANT IN HER PAINTING.

Emily Kame Kngwarreye was born in c.1910. For most of her early and adult life INDIGENOUS, ABORIGINAL AND TORRES STRAIT ISLANDER PEOPLES' LANDS were controlled by EUROPEAN SETTLERS.

Emily Kame Kngwarreye was an elder of the ANMATYERR PEOPLE from the north of Uluru. She looked after the women's Dreaming sites of Alhalkere.

In 1976, Aboriginal LAND RIGHTS WERE AGREED by law and First Nations communities could prove ownership of their land. In 1978, Emily along with other women of the Utopia Community set up the UTOPIA WOMEN'S BATIK GROUP to explore stories of the landscape and rituals of their people.

Emily often painted using BIG DAUBS OF PAINT, rather than neat familiar dots often used by other artists. Her bold style was very particular to her.

52

Emily painted
**EARTH'S CREATION** when
she was 84. She draws on the
spirits' creation of both land and
people. She used lots of **GREEN** to
suggest the **RAINS** that make the
**DESERT OF CENTRAL AUSTRALIA**
come alive with a burst of
spectacular colour.

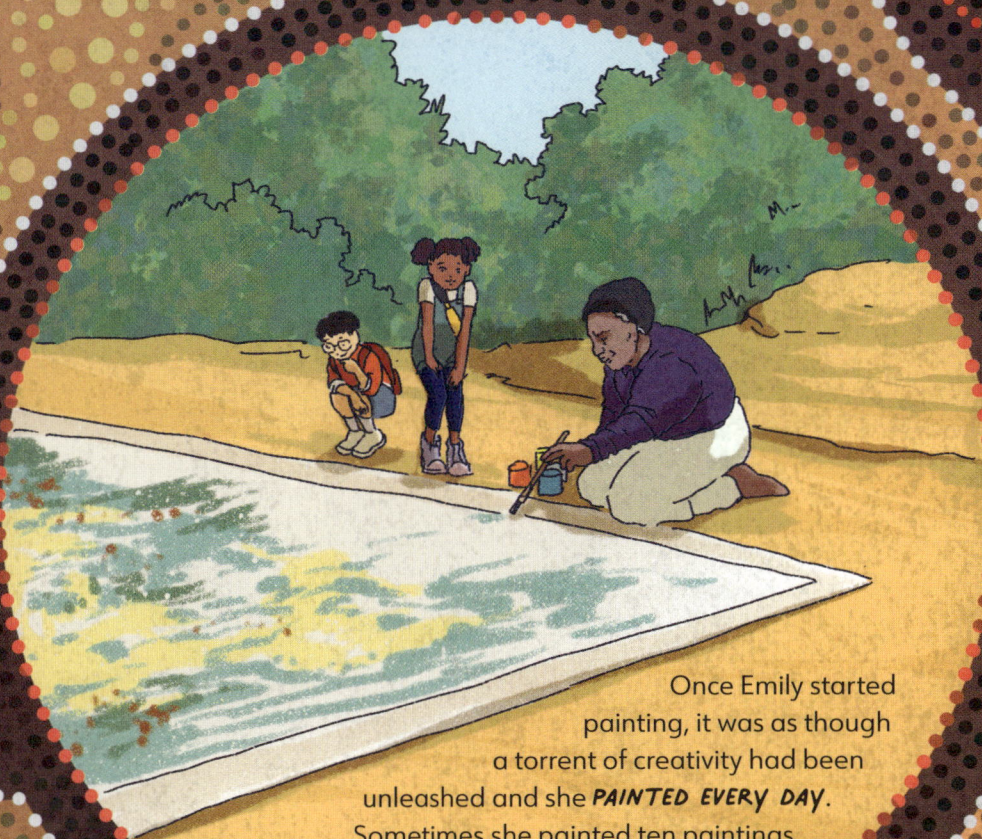

Once Emily started
painting, it was as though
a torrent of creativity had been
unleashed and she **PAINTED EVERY DAY**.
Sometimes she painted ten paintings
in a day and other times, her larger
paintings could take many,
many days to finish.

**EARTH'S CREATION, 1994**

Emily didn't try to paint the shapes of the animals and heroes of the **DREAMTIME CREATION STORY**. Instead she used paint in **DOTS AND SWIRLS**, to show the **ENERGY AND JOY** of that event and its amazing ability to support us all, even thousands of years later.

1994

# TOKYO, JAPAN

## KEY ARTIST: YAYOI KUSAMA

YAYOI KUSAMA IS A CONTEMPORARY JAPANESE ARTIST WHO EXPLORES IDEAS FROM IDENTITY TO INFINITY IN HER COLOURFUL AND OFTEN LARGE-SCALE WORKS. BORN IN MATSUMOTO, NAGANO, A CITY SURROUNDED BY MOUNTAINS. HER PARENTS OWNED A SEED FARM AND PLANT NURSERY AND SHE WORKED IN A PARACHUTE FACTORY AS A TEENAGER DURING THE SECOND WORLD WAR. AS AN ADULT SHE LEFT HER HOME COUNTRY AND MOVED TO NEW YORK. YOU CAN SEE ALL OF THESE INFLUENCES IN HER WORK FROM NATURAL FORMS TO THE BRIGHT COLOURS OF AMERICAN POP ART IN THE 1960S. FOR THE LAST 40 YEARS, SHE HAS CHOSEN TO LIVE IN A PSYCHIATRIC HOSPITAL IN TOKYO, AND EACH DAY SHE WORKS AT HER NEARBY STUDIO. KUSAMA SAYS SHE FEELS LIKE AN OUTSIDER AND THAT CREATING ART IS HER WAY TO ESCAPE.

The *PUMPKIN* sits on the edge of a wharf overlooking the Seto Inland Sea in Japan on the amazing *NAOSHIMA ISLAND* – a place which celebrates nature, art and architecture.

YAYOI KUSAMA IS INSTANTLY *RECOGNISABLE* in her *BRIGHT RED WIG.* Her phenomenal output has astonished the art world and today she is regarded as one of the *MOST SUCCESSFUL ARTISTS IN THE WORLD* and her exhibitions have drawn record-breaking crowds. She is open and brave about *FACING MENTAL ILLNESS.* The way she uses art as a comfort which delights the rest of the world is very *POWERFUL AND INSPIRING.*

PUMPKIN, 1994

Yayoi has celebrated both the shape of the pumpkin and its markings by creating *ROWS AND ROWS OF BLACK DOTS OF DIFFERENT SIZES.* These emphasise the *CONTOURS* of the pumpkin. The yellow dots on the *BLACK STALK* look a bit *LIKE A TOP HAT*: a cheeky cherry on top of the sculpture!

Lots of Kusama's work uses *DOTS AND LIGHT* so that she can make you think about ideas which keep *REPEATING THEMSELVES*, just like the minutes, hours and days of our lives.

Yayoi Kusama arrived in New York just as *ANDY WARHOL, ROY LICHTENSTEIN* and *CLAES OLDENBURG* were experimenting with a new style which became known as *POP ART*. These artists wanted to take objects from our ordinary lives and recreate them using *MODERN MANUFACTURING METHODS*.

The *WATERFRONT LOCATION* makes us think about the relationship between *PEOPLE AND NATURE*. The *GIANT SCALE* and bright colour literally brightens your day. Maybe it also makes you think of *MAGIC AND FAIRY TALES* – where things can take on new sizes and even have their own superpowers?!

If this were a real pumpkin it would rot away. This pumpkin is made from *PAINTED FIBREGLASS* so that it will stay *SHINY AND BRIGHT*, whatever the weather outside. Contemporary art like this plays with different meanings all at the same time – *WHAT DOES THIS SCULPTURE MAKE YOU THINK OF?*

IF YOU LIKE PLAYFUL WORKS LIKE THIS, HAVE A LOOK AT TAKASHI MURAKAMI'S ART. HE MIXES IDEAS FROM TRADITIONAL JAPANESE ART WITH WESTERN STYLES, TO CREATE WORKS WHICH ARE POPULAR RIGHT ACROSS THE WORLD TODAY. SEE IF YOU CAN SPOT THE LINKS TO ANIME (COMICS) AND MANGA (ANIMATED FILMS) IN HIS WORK. MURAKAMI'S HUGE SUCCESS HAS ALLOWED HIM TO EMPLOY LOTS OF PEOPLE TO HELP HIM IN HIS STUDIO.

# 2007
# LIVERPOOL, UK

## KEY ARTISTS: THE SINGH TWINS

WE ALL NEED TO FEEL A SENSE OF BELONGING TO AND PRIDE IN A PLACE AND A COMMUNITY. IN LIVERPOOL AT THE BEGINNING OF THE 21ST CENTURY, THE BRITISH ARTISTS, THE SINGH TWINS, SHOWED THIS IN A NEW PAINTING STYLE THEY CALLED 'PAST MODERN'. THE CITY OF LIVERPOOL IS AN IMPORTANT CULTURAL CENTRE WITH MORE MUSEUMS AND GALLERIES THAN ANY UK CITY OUTSIDE LONDON. THE BROAD RANGE OF THE PEOPLE WHO LIVE THERE REFLECT THE RICH AND INTERESTING WORLD IN WHICH WE LIVE. WHEN LIVERPOOL WAS CHOSEN TO BECOME EUROPE'S CITY OF CULTURE IN 2008, THE SINGH TWINS PAINTED THEIR VISION OF THE CITY, WHICH NOW HANGS IN THE FAMOUS ST GEORGE'S HALL.

This painting draws on the twins' *INDIAN HERITAGE* and the *MINIATURE ART* made famous by the Persians and Mughals hundreds of years ago. The picture is filled with references that define Liverpool.

In the middle is a re-imagined version of the *CITY'S COAT OF ARMS*. On the left Neptune symbolises the achievements of Liverpool in different fields. The tattoo on his chest spells *'SCHOOL' IN BRAILLE* to remember Britain's first school for the blind in Liverpool in 1791.

The buildings of the city span a curving horizon that looks like the edge of the Earth. Here you can spot *THE GREAT ALBERT DOCK* (at the time such a *FEAT OF ENGINEERING* that it was compared to the great pyramids of Egypt).

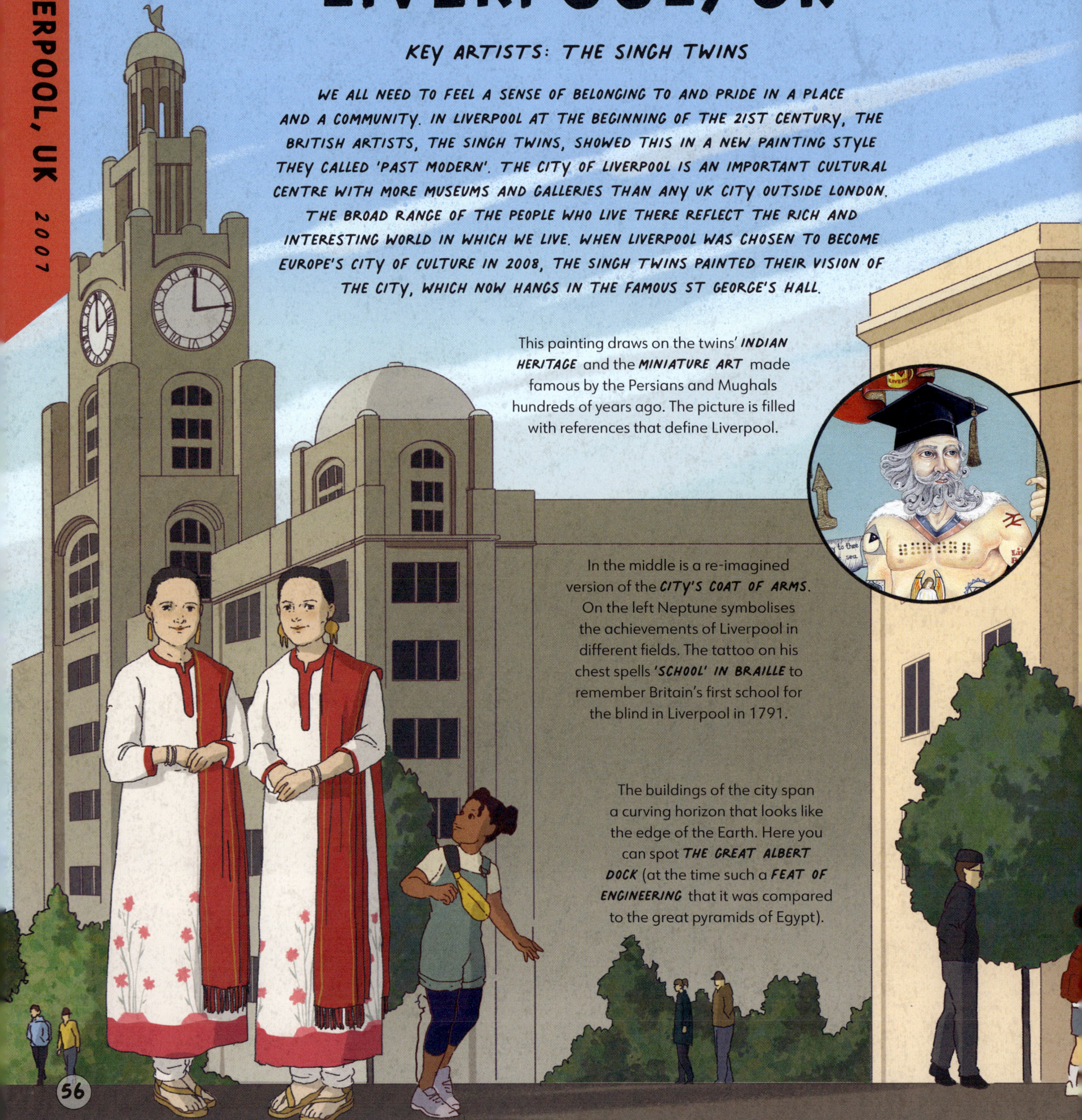

56

THE STATUE OF LIBERTY to the left and a CHINESE PAGODA on the far right show the GLOBAL IMPORTANCE OF THE PORT OF LIVERPOOL. Can you find the Blue Funnel steamship which was the first to trade with the Far East?

TO THE RIGHT OF THE CREST, Triton holds a microphone to show Liverpool's great MUSICAL HISTORY. After all, this is the home of THE BEATLES!

## LIVERPOOL 800: THE CHANGING FACE OF LIVERPOOL, 2007

IN THE CENTRAL CREST, the patterns show all the COMMUNITIES who have built the city together: Africans, Greeks, South Asians, Persians, Chinese, Irish and Europeans. ONE PIECE OF THE PUZZLE IS STILL EMPTY: who will help shape the city in the 21st century?

IN THE CENTRE OF THE CREST, the famous LIVERBIRD holds a PEN and BRUSH instead of the traditional SEAWEED. This is to show that the city's future is a creative one rather than a maritime one.

CAN YOU FIND AN X-RAY IN THIS PAINTING? The first use of an X-ray in Britain was on a 12-year-old-boy in a Liverpool hospital by Charles Thurston-Holland.

YOU ENTER THE PAINTING AT THE BOTTOM, through the GATEWAY of Calderstones Park. Above the gateway is an ANGLO-SAXON BROOCH, VIKING SHIP and IRON BRIDGE, which add to the layers of ANCIENT HISTORY that make up THE CITY'S IDENTITY.

Ai Weiwei made this **HUGE SCULPTURE** called *LAW OF THE JOURNEY* in 2018. When he showed it in Prague in the Czech Republic, it made people think carefully about *HUMAN DIGNITY* and *HUMAN RIGHTS*. The anonymous figures symbolise the millions of *REFUGEES* who have *ESCAPED DANGEROUS PLACES* by a risky sea journey.

Ai's **70-METRE BOAT SCULPTURE** carries more than **300** FIGURES a bit like *A MODERN NOAH'S ARK* (a story from the bible and the Qur'an). The boat hangs overhead, making the viewers in the room feel that this problem is enormous and *OVERSHADOWS US ALL*.

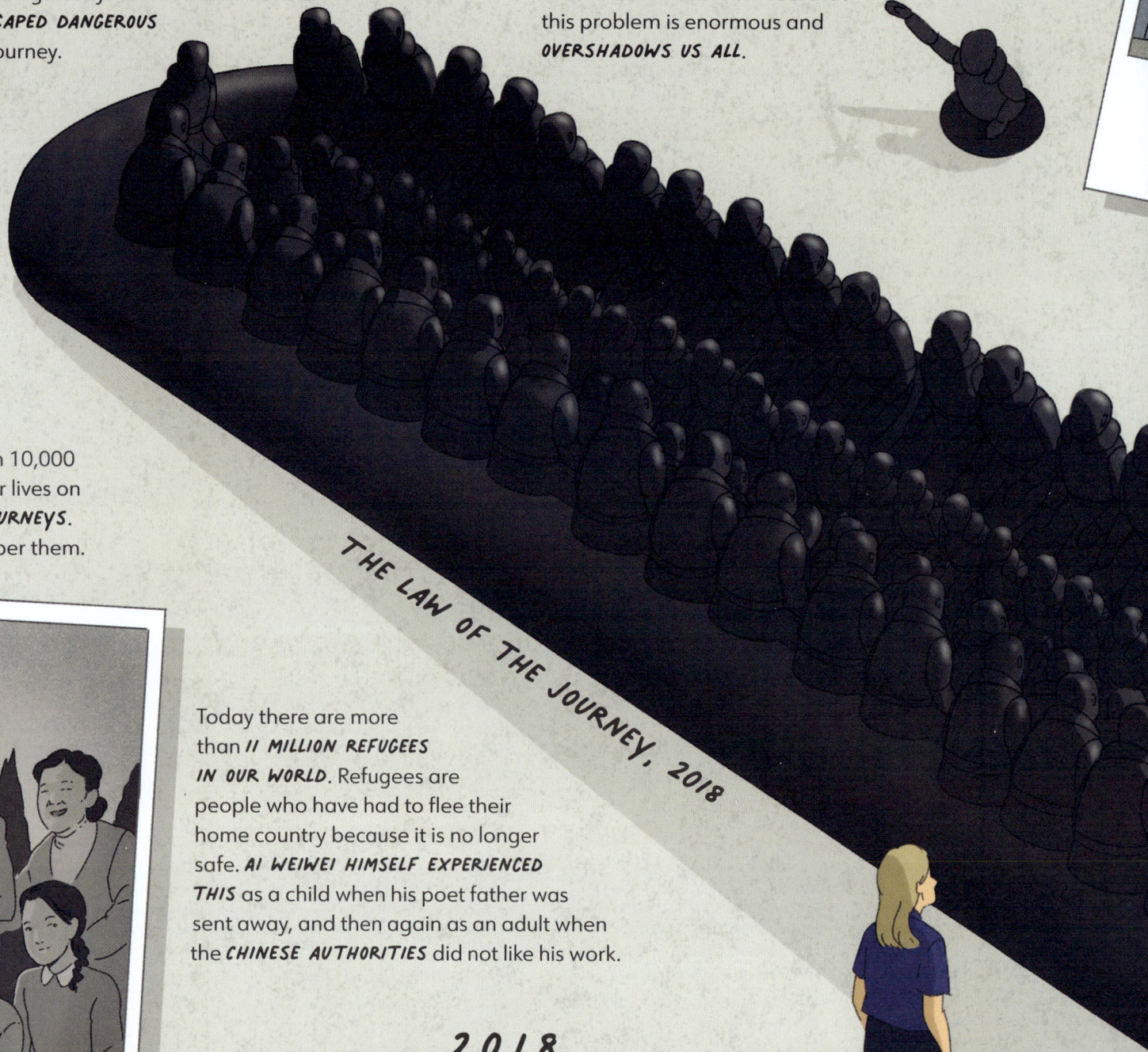

Tragically, more than 10,000 people have lost their lives on these *DANGEROUS JOURNEYS*. Ai helps us to remember them.

*THE LAW OF THE JOURNEY, 2018*

Today there are more than *11 MILLION REFUGEES IN OUR WORLD*. Refugees are people who have had to flee their home country because it is no longer safe. *AI WEIWEI HIMSELF EXPERIENCED THIS* as a child when his poet father was sent away, and then again as an adult when the *CHINESE AUTHORITIES* did not like his work.

# 2018
# PRAGUE, CZECH REPUBLIC

## KEY ARTIST: AI WEIWEI

JOURNEYS HAVE ALWAYS BEEN IMPORTANT: TO MAKE SOMETHING SPECIAL, ARTISTS NEED TO BE OPEN-MINDED, DETERMINED AND SENSITIVE. IN OUR MODERN, GLOBAL WORLD, CHALLENGES AND IDEAS ARE NOT LIMITED TO ONE PLACE OR ONE MOMENT, BUT AFFECT ALL OF US AT THE SAME TIME. CHINESE ARTIST AI WEIWEI IS SHOCKED AND SADDENED BY THE SUFFERING OF SO MANY PEOPLE IN OUR WORLD. HE IS DETERMINED TO USE HIS ART TO DRIVE FORWARD CHANGE FOR THE BETTER.

**THE BUILDING** that this work is in is important too. It was once used to celebrate international trade in 1928. But during the **SECOND WORLD WAR**, thousands of **CZECH JEWS** were held here before they were deported on a different unwanted journey, to the nearby concentration camp at Terezin.

Ai Weiwei's artwork is powerful because it reminds us that **OUR WORLD IS INTERCONNECTED**, and we are all in it together. Everyone deserves safe haven and safe travels.

Every part of this sculpture was made from **BLACK RUBBER** in a **FACTORY IN CHINA**. The factory also manufactures the actual rubber boats that many refugees use to escape. In this way, Ai makes both the **MATERIALS AND THE MAKING** of his art an important **PART OF THE MESSAGE**.

Because the figures have **NO NAMES OR FACES**, they represent **ALL PEOPLE**, young or old, women or men, who have experienced war and being displaced.

YOUR ACTIONS HAVE A BIG IMPACT ON OTHERS. IF YOU WELCOME NEWCOMERS TO YOUR VILLAGE OR SCHOOL YOU COULD CHANGE THEIR WORLD FOR EVER...

The title **THE LAW OF THE JOURNEY** is a reference to the **WRITING OF FRANZ KAFKA**. He too explored the importance of journeys and the connections we all make between start and end points as well as the unexpected detours that often happen.

# GLOSSARY

**ACTIVIST** A person who campaigns to bring about political or social change.

**ARCHITECT** A person who designs buildings.

**ARTEFACT** An object, ornament or tool that is made by a human being and is of historical or cultural interest.

**ASTRONOMY** A branch of science that is the study of everything in the universe beyond the Earth's atmosphere.

**BAROQUE** A style of art, music and architecture from Europe from the 17th and 18th centuries. It is usually dramatic and filled with detail.

**BCE** A system of numbering years in the ancient period 'Before common era'. In Christianity, it stands for 'Before Christian era'.

**BRAILLE** A system of writing for blind or visually impaired people. Is is made from raised dots and the reader uses their fingertips to feel the words. Invented by Louis Braille.

**CALLIGRAPHY** The art of creating and designing lettering, usually with a pen or brush and ink.

**CE** 'Common Era'. The system of numbering years starting from the beginning of the common era. In Christianity, this is also referred to as 'AD', or *anno Domini*, meaning 'year of our lord' in Latin.

**CENTAUR** A creature from Greek mythology. It has the lower body of a horse and upper body of a man.

**CERAMICS** A fine art and craft that includes shaping pottery, stoneware and earthenware clay fired in an oven called a kiln.

**COAT OF ARMS** Usually associated with a particular family or group, this is an image of a shield with symbols, colours and creatures arranged on it.

**COMPOSER** A person who writes pieces of music.

**COLONISATION** The action or process of settling among and establishing control over the native or indigenous people of an area.

**DECOLONISATION** When a country that was previously colonised becomes independent. It can refer to the process of undoing practises or behaviours that became accepted during the colonial period.

**DEMOCRACY** A system of government whereby the people in a country vote to decide on who is in charge.

**DREAMTIME** This is the foundation of Indigenous Australian, Aboriginal and Torres Strait Islander religion, and cultures. It is the period of creation by ancestral spirits and the origin of all knowledge. It is ongoing and exists in the past, present and will continue to exist into the future.

**DYNASTY** A series of rulers or leaders who are all from the same family, or a period when a country is ruled by them.

**ELDER** An older member of a society or community who is respected, in part for their wisdom.

**ELITE** A small but powerful group of people.

**EMPIRE** When a country controls other countries or states beyond their own borders this is an empire. This practice is called Imperialism.

**FLEET** A group of ships.

**INDIGENOUS** People who have inhabited a place from a time before colonisers or settlers arrived.

**INSTALLATION** A type of three-dimensional visual art that usually takes up a whole room or space and requires the viewer to move through or around it.

**LAPIS LAZULI** A bright blue mineral which can be ground into a pigment to make blue paint. Used especially in the 13th and 14th centuries. It was very expensive and so was often used as a display of wealth and luxury.

**MENORAH** A seven-armed candle holder used in Jewish worship. A nine-armed holder is called a Chanukiah and is lit during the celebration of Hanukkah.

**MIGRATION** The movement of people as they leave one place to go to another.

**MINARET** A type of tower that is usually attached to a Mosque and is used to project the Muslim call to prayer.

**MONUMENT** A public building, structure or sculpture that has particular significance to commemorate or memorialise a person or event.

**PAN-AFRICAN MOVEMENT** A political movement with the aim of establishing independence for African countries and fostering solidarity among African people around the world.

**PIGMENT** The substance in paint that gives it colour.

**POP ART** An art movement that emerged in the late 1950s in particular in the UK and USA. It often uses bright colours and references popular, or 'pop', culture.

**QU'RAN** A sacred book and the main religious text in Islam.

**REFUGEE** A person or group of people who has been forced to leave their country to escape war, persecution or natural disaster.

**RELIEF SCULPTURE** A sculpture that sticks out from, or projects, from a flat background.

**RENAISSANCE** Meaning 'rebirth', this was a period of time from the 14th to 17th centuries in Europe. It was marked by the revival in an interest in Classical wisdom and learning.

**SLAVERY** A situation where people are owned by others, or held under their complete control, with no ability to leave. They are forced to obey and treated as objects that can be bought, sold and exploited.

**SONGLINES** In indigenous Australian Aboriginal cultures, these are sacred spiritual pathways across the land and sky. They are also known as dreaming tracks. They trace the paths of ancestral spirits who created the world.

**STELE** A carved slab of stone often used in ancient cultures as a grave or a way of commemorating an important event or story.

**SYMBOL** Something (often an image) that represents or stands for something else.

**UNDERWORLD** Existing in different forms in many cultures around the world, this is the mythical world of the dead, often imagined to be under the ground.

**UTOPIA** An imagined place in which everything is perfect. It is also the name of an Indigenous Community in Australia's Northern Territory.

# FURTHER READING

If you want to read more about the things covered in this book or if you want to discover even more about the history of art, here is a list of useful sources including books and websites you might find interesting.

## BOOKS

*A History of Pictures for Children,* David Hockney, Martin Gayford and Rose Blake, Thames & Hudson (2018)

*Black Artists Shaping the World,* Sharna Jackson and Zoe Whitley, Thames & Hudson (2021)

*How Art Works,* Sarah Hull, Usborne (2020)

*I Know An Artist: The Inspiring Connections Between the World's Greatest Artists,* Susie Hodge and Sarah Papworth, White Lion (2019)

*The Ultimate Art Museum,* Ferren Gipson, Phaidon (2011)

*Vincent's Starry Night and Other Stories: A Children's History of Art,* Michael Bird and Kate Evans, Laurence King Publishing (2016)

*Why is Art Full of Naked People? And Other Vital Questions About Art,* Susie Hodge and Claire Goble, Thames & Hudson (2016)

## WEBSITES

Tate Kids from the Tate Gallery in London: tate.org.uk/kids

Met Kids from the Metropolitan Museum of Art: metmuseum.org/art/online-features/metkids/

## MORE ADVENTURES FROM WIDE EYED EDITIONS:

*Atlas of Lost Kingdoms: Discover Mythical Lands, Lost Islands and Vanished Cities,* Emily Hawkins and Lauren Baldo (2022)

*Atlas of Adventures: Wonders of the World,* Emily Hawkins and Lucy Letherland (2018)

*Music is My Life: Soundtrack Your Life with 80 Artists for Every Occasion*, Myles Tanzer and Ali Mac (2019)

*Planet Fashion: 100 Years of Fashion History,* Natasha Slee and Cynthia Kittler (2018)

# IMAGE CREDITS

*FOR MY MUM; AND TOM, ROSIE, INDI AND MAX: THANK YOU FOR BEING MY CONSTANT SOURCE OF INSPIRATION — S.P.*

*A Whole World of Art* © 2023 Quarto Publishing plc.
Text © 2023 Sarah Phillips
Illustrations © 2023 Dion Mehaga Bangun Djayasaputra

First Published in 2023 by Wide Eyed Editions,
an imprint of The Quarto Group, 1 Triptych Place, London, SE1 9SH.
T (0)20 7700 6700 F (0)20 7700 8066 **www.Quarto.com**

A catalogue record for this book is available from the British Library.

ISBN 978-0-7112-6536-3
eISBN 978-0-7112-6538-7

The illustrations were created digitally
Set in Palmer Lake Print and URW Form

Published by Debbie Foy
Commissioned by Lucy Brownridge
Designed by Kate Haynes and Sophie Stericker
Production by Dawn Cameron
Picture research by Poppy David

Manufactured in Malaysia CO062023

9 8 7 6 5 4 3 2 1

MIX
Paper | Supporting responsible forestry
FSC
www.fsc.org FSC™ C007207